FIORENZA

CASSELL CARAVEL BOOKS

A CASSELL CARAVEL BOOK

LORENZO DE' MEDICI
AND THE RENAISSANCE

By the Editors of
HORIZON MAGAZINE

Author
CHARLES L. MEE

Consultant
JOHN WALKER
Director, National Gallery of Art, Washington, D.C.

Cassell · London

© 1969 by American Heritage Publishing Co., Inc., 551 Fifth Avenue, New York, New
York 10017. All rights reserved under Berne and Pan-American Copyright Conventions.
Trademark CARAVEL registered United States Patent Office
First published in Great Britain 1971
I.S.B.N. 0 304 93682 0

In Lorenzo's time the Piazza della Signoria was the center of Florentine life and government.

FOREWORD

We tend to view our historical figures as being of a gray, indeterminate middle age, or we recall them as old men, their work done, their great days past, their lives divested of all but the echoing legends. Lorenzo de' Medici, however, was never an old man; he died in 1492, the year of America's discovery, at the age of forty-three. He came to power in fifteenth-century Florence as a very young man of twenty. In the twenty-odd years of his rule, this young man—this banker, this politician, this international diplomat, this free-wheeling, lusty poet and writer of songs, this Establishment-member and energetic revolutionary—helped to give shape and tone and tempo to that truly dazzling time of Western history, the Renaissance.

Lorenzo lived during the very apex of the Renaissance, and his life and his thought touched nearly all who lived in his age: Michelangelo, Botticelli, Leonardo, the Strozzi and Pitti families in Florence, the Sforza in Milan, the kings of Naples, the popes in Rome. He dined with them, drank with them, fought with them. He had "a zest for all of life," as our author remarks, "so vigorous and infectious that he drew his age about him and dominated it by the sheer force of his character. Indeed, his talents and enthusiasms were so all-encompassing that he stands as an archetype of 'the Renaissance man.'"

In the pages that follow is the story of his brief whirlwind life and of the times in which he lived. No other age has been documented by so many brilliant artists as the Renaissance, and Lorenzo's story is illustrated here by his contemporaries and his friends.

What has it to do with us? As any history does, of course, it enriches our own experience. But this particular history may seem particularly apt today. For the Renaissance was a time in which old values and traditions were under attack, when young artists demolished old standards and established new ones, when men gazed toward the past to look for guidelines to use in their own tumultuous, chaotic, and confusing world. It was a time of dismay and anxiety, of restlessness, riot, and despair. That such a time can turn out so well may reassure us—especially if we learn from the men who helped to make the Renaissance an age not only of endings but also of hope and of great achievement.

THE EDITORS

CONTENTS

I THE RISE OF THE MEDICI

The murderers being ready, each in his appointed station, which they could retain without any suspicion, on account of the vast numbers assembled in the church, the preconcerted moment arrived, and Bernardo Bandini, with a short dagger . . ., struck Giuliano in the breast, who, after a few steps, fell to the earth. Francesco de' Pazzi threw himself upon the body and covered him with wounds; whilst, as if blinded by rage, he inflicted a deep incision upon his own leg. Antonio and Stefano the priest attacked Lorenzo, and after dealing many blows, effected only a slight incision in the throat; for either their want of resolution, the activity of Lorenzo, who, finding himself attacked, used his arms in his own defense, or the assistance of those by whom he was surrounded, rendered all attempts futile. They fled. . . .

Thus the wily Italian diplomat and historian Niccolò Machiavelli described the fateful day of the Pazzi conspir-

Although the fifteenth-century manuscript illustration to the left purports to depict the sacking of Troy by the Greeks in Vergil's Aeneid, the artist apparently had in mind the civil disorders that accompanied the power struggles of the Medici in Florence. Indeed, the massive, fortresslike building prominent in the picture is a facsimile of the Medici palace.

Lorenzo commissioned Bertoldo di Giovanni to design and forge this bronze medallion in honor of his dead brother. On one side (left) Lorenzo escapes behind an altar. On the other, Giuliano is slain.

acy—Sunday morning, April 26, 1478. A typical little tale of the Renaissance? Well, not quite. It was, to be sure, a time of violence and bloodshed, a time for soaring ambition and bitter rivalry, for intense hatreds and transcendent loves. It was, in short, a time for great passions. And murder, even murder in a cathedral, even a murder for which the cue was the ringing of the bells at the most sacred moment of the Mass, must not seem too exceptional.

What was exceptional, however, was the intended victim of the conspiracy. One need only identify the Lorenzo spoken of in order to lend historic importance to the moment. He was Lorenzo de' Medici, the most remarkable of all the remarkable Medici family. To so distinguish him is no faint praise, for the Medici were the leading family in Florence, and Florence was the leading city in Italy during that period of most dazzling achievement, the Renaissance. In that brilliant family, in that astonishing town, in that age of surpassing magnificence, Lorenzo was called The Magnificent.

He was a robust man, with a strong athletic body, and a zest for all of life so vigorous and infectious that he drew his age about him and dominated it by the sheer force of his character. Indeed, his talents and enthusiasms were so all-encompassing that he stands as an archetype of "the Renaissance Man."

Lorenzo escaped the assassins—with only a minor gash in his neck—by wrapping his cloak around his forearm, drawing his sword, and fighting his way to the sacristy, where the massive bronze doors closed behind him with an echoing clang. Fearing that the assassin's dagger might have been poisoned, a friend sucked the wound, and Lorenzo managed to get back to his palace with little more incident.

His brother, Giuliano, however, was dead. He had been attacked with such fury that it was discovered later that his body had been ripped by twenty-nine dagger blows.

The assassins had expected the citizens of Florence to rise up and join them. They were fatally wrong, as this excerpt from the diary of shopkeeper Luca Landucci indicates:

Meantime all the city was up in arms, in the piazza and at Lorenzo de' Medici's house. And numbers of men on the side of the conspirators were killed in the piazza, amongst others a priest of the bishop's was killed there, his body being quartered and the head cut off, and then the head was stuck on the top of a lance, and carried about Florence the whole day, and one quarter of his body was carried on a spit all through the city, with the cry of: 'Death to the traitors!' . . .
The next day they hung Jacopo Salviati . . . and the other Jacopo, also at the windows, and many others of the households of the cardinal and of the bishop. And the day after that . . . Messrs. Jacopo de' Pazzi and Renato de' Pazzi were hung at the windows of the *Palazzo Signoria* . . . and so many of their men with them, that during these three days the number of those killed amounted to more than seventy.

Revenge for the death of Giuliano—and for the attempt on Lorenzo's life—did not cease until two hundred seventy conspirators were killed, exiled, or ruined. After the body of Jacopo de' Pazzi had been buried, our shopkeeper reports,

some boys disinterred it . . . and dragged it through Florence by the piece of rope that was still round its neck. . . . And when they grew tired and did not know what more to do with it, they . . . threw it into the river. . . . And it was considered an extraordinary thing, first because children are usually afraid of dead bodies, and secondly because the stench was so bad that it was impossible to go near it; one may imagine what it was like [after twenty days]. And they must have had to touch it with their hands to throw it into the Arno. And as it floated down the river, always keeping above the surface, the bridges were crowded with people to watch it pass. . . .

Thus the old man Jacopo de' Pazzi, whose family had tried to kill Lorenzo, was sent to sea.

The Pazzi name was stricken from the public records, the family's coat of arms was torn from buildings, and the intersection Canto de' Pazzi was given a new name. For the death of one Medici, not merely the death of seventy, but the extinction of the very name of Pazzi.

The Florentines surpassed most men, surely, in their appetite for violence. Yet they surpassed most men as well in

Young Leonardo da Vinci sketched the conspirator Bernardo Bandini hanging from a window of Florence's Palazzo della Signoria.

As commerce began to thrive in Renaissance Italy, hitherto sleepy towns bustled with activity. The daily comings and goings of tradesmen and workers in Siena were recorded by Ambrogio Lorenzetti in this fresco for Siena's town hall.

their hunger for great achievements. Across the street from the *duomo*, or cathedral, where the assassination took place, was the Baptistery, its doors adorned with bronze reliefs sculpted by Lorenzo Ghiberti. Ghiberti took twenty-seven years to complete the doors; a younger artist, Michelangelo, later called them "fit to be the Gates of Paradise."

Florence, then, was a city where men could make the Gates of Paradise or behave like the very denizens of hell. The Florentines knew the full range of human experience, and they delighted in expressing all of it—in poetry, in painting, in sculpture and architecture, in politics and business, and even in murder. How it came to be a city stuffed with the greatest and meanest of human passions, and how the Medici came to dominate it, requires some brief rehearsal of history.

In the Middle Ages the landscape of Italy was one in which great fortified castles perched atop the country's thousands of mountain peaks. The land around was devoted

almost exclusively to agriculture, farmed by serfs who vir-
tually were owned, body and soul, by the feudal lords who
ruled their miniature kingdoms from their castles.

In about A.D. 1000 everything began to change. Commerce revived—first in trade with the East, and then
throughout Europe. With commerce, towns came to be
filled with traders and merchants, clothmakers and bankers, and craftsmen of all descriptions.

They were a new breed of men: self-made, ambitious,
and fiercely independent. Their first job, as they saw it, was
to get rid of the feudal lords and nobles. They got rid of the
nobles, strangely enough, by lending them money.

Beginning as what amounted to small-time pawnbrokers,
the new men took as security on their loans the nobles' vast
feudal estates. When the nobles were unable to pay their
debts on time, the moneylenders lent more money—taking
more land as security and charging higher interest rates.
The interest rates commonly ran as high as thirty and forty

15

per cent; it was usury with a vengeance. Finally, the pawn-brokers had amassed large fortunes and risen to the status of great bankers—and gradually they divested the nobles altogether of their estates. Over the course of two or three centuries nearly all the nobles were reduced to helpless paupers.

Banking was a fast-paced, risky business, and most merchant-banking companies lasted only a single generation before stupidity, overambition, or mere bad luck ruined them. Those who survived were tough, proud men. The toughest, smartest, and luckiest of them all were the Florentines, and they made Florence the leading cloth-trading and banking city in Italy. The city was, to put it crudely, the garment district and the Wall Street of Italy.

By 1400, the Italian peninsula was divided into a number of city-states, dominated by five major powers: the Papal States, Venice, Milan, Naples, and Florence. In addition to his spiritual realm, the pope in Rome ruled as temporal lord of a sizable portion of central Italy. Venice was a police state, ruled by an oligarchy; Naples was governed by a king; and Milan was dominated by a tyrannical prince, whose coat of arms bore a coiled serpent, in its mouth a beet-red human body having its life choked out. Florence alone was a democracy, dominated, to be sure, by its leading merchant-banking families, but a democracy nonetheless.

Historians never will cease to debate just what the Italian Renaissance was and exactly how, and how much, it differed from the Middle Ages and the period that followed it, when it began, and when it ended. But it is possible to say precisely when the Renaissance began in Florence: in the year 1402.

In 1390, heralds of the ambitious Duke of Milan appeared in Florence and announced the Duke's intention of ruling all Italy for himself. A chilling declaration, it sent Florence searching wildly for allies to oppose Milan. "One by one," as a modern historian has written, "the allies of Florence deserted her. One by one the last city republics of Italy surrendered their liberties to the great Duke, until Florence stood alone, surrounded and at bay." Exhausted, ravaged by famine, and losing as many as two hundred citizens a day to the plague, the present was a nightmare, and Florentines began to gaze longingly at the past. It was then, in 1400, that the scholar Leonardo Bruni wrote his *Praise of Florence*, characterizing Florence as a bastion of liberty, the inheritor and preserver of the values of the civilizations of antiquity.

BIBLIOTHÈQUE NATIONALE, PARIS

Like the Albizzi and Medici families in Florence, the Visconti ruled Milan. This figure holds two versions of the Visconti emblem—a man-eating serpent.

16

"To the desperate Florentines," the modern historian adds, "the great comet which flamed across the heavens in the spring of 1402 must have seemed to portend the death of Italian freedom. Instead it announced the death of the great Duke." With the death of the Duke, the forces of Milan fell apart, retreated, and left Florence intact. The Florentines felt, and much of Italy agreed, that their moral courage established them as champions of freedom, a city populated by heroic individuals, the likes of whom had not been seen since the days of ancient Greece and Rome. The Florentines knew that with that victory they had entered a new era.

It was from this atmosphere of cutthroat business, rugged individualism, and soaring ideals that the Medici family emerged in Florence. To survive in this heady and hazardous atmosphere required both daring and caution. By 1402, the dawn of the most vigorous century in Florence, there were two chief rival merchant-banking families in Florence: the Albizzi and the Medici. The Albizzi had all the aggressiveness, and the Medici, for the time being, had all the patience.

The first Medici of whom we need take notice is Salvestro, who once served as Gonfalonier of Justice, the highest public office in Florence. In 1378, according to the modern historian Ferdinand Schevill, "he instigated a successful coup against a group of high-born political manipulators, thereby winning standing and reputation . . . as a friend of the people. From Salvestro's time the humbler Florentines . . . were firmly persuaded that the Medici were the one major guild clan which could be counted on to champion their cause." For Salvestro's pains, as the Albizzi rose to greater and greater power, his branch of the Medici family sank lower and lower among the families of Florence, ultimately disappearing altogether from history.

On the other hand, the supremely shrewd Giovanni di Bicci de' Medici was finding a place of prominence among the wealthy men of Florence. Born in 1360, Giovanni di Bicci was the first notable member of Lorenzo's branch of the family; his advice to his descendants was, "Be as inconspicuous as possible."

Giovanni remained carefully aloof from politics, lived modestly, probably initiated the Medici habit of lying on tax returns, and thus avoided having his property taken by the Albizzi. He spent his time quietly amassing a fortune and managed to become banker to the Pope and his court at Rome, an account of pivotal importance to the Medici for-

REPUBLIC OF

Trent

Feltre

Lake
Como

Asolo

COLLEONI

Bergamo

Lake
Garda

Verona

Vicenza

Venice

Brescia

Padua

Chiogg

LOMBARDY

Milan

SFORZA   VISCONTI

Lodi

Pavia

Cremona

MINCIO RIVER

GONZAGA   Mantua

ADIGE RIVER

Ferrara

D. ESTE   FERRARA

DUCHY OF
MILAN

PO RIVER

MANTUA

Mirandola

BENTIVOGLIO

Parma

Modena

Fornovo

Bologna   Imola

Faenza   For

DUCHY
OF
MODENA

Genoa

REPUBLIC OF
GENOA

Sarzana

Carrara

REPUBLIC
OF LUCCA

Lucca

Pistoia

Prato

Fiesole

Florence

MEDICI

REPUBLIC OF
FLORENCE

GULF OF
GENOA

Pisa

ARNO RIVER

TUSCANY

Livorno

PETRUCCI

Volterra

Siena

REPUBLIC
OF
SIENA

ELBA

CORSICA

David Greenspan

RENAISSANCE ITALY

By the fifteenth century, the five major powers of Italy—Venice, Milan, Naples, Florence, and the Papal States—had divided the peninsula into a number of small, independent states. Constantly at war with one another, many of the states were ruled by wealthy banking families. The coats of arms of several of the important families— as well as some of the notable palaces and cathedrals of Renaissance Italy—are shown on this map.

Trieste

ENICE

venna

ROMAGNA

MALATESTA

Rimini

Pesaro

Fano

San Marino

Sinigaglia

Ancona

Borgo San Sepolcro

Urbino

DA MONTEFELTRO

THE MARCHES

Anghiari

zo

BAGLIONE

Perugia

Assisi

Lake Trasimeno

STATES OF THE CHURCH

nza

Orvieto

TIBER RIVER

Aquila

Lake Bolsena

Viterbo

KINGDOM OF NAPLES

Tivoli

ADRIATIC SEA

Rome

COLONNA

THE PAPACY

ORSINI

Benevento

Ostia

ARAGON

Naples

Amalfi

TYRRHENIAN SEA

ISCHIA

tunes. Henceforth ninety per cent of Medici wealth would come from banking, half their banking profits and most of their working capital from Rome. The tax records probably are accurate on one point: in the report for 1403 Giovanni ranked twenty-first in his quarter of the city in wealth; in the report of 1427, he is listed as the richest man in his quarter.

If the Albizzi realized what a powerful man had grown up inconspicuously in their midst, they were unable to do anything about it. The stolid Giovanni gave them no cause. He served once, and only once, as Gonfalonier of Justice, in 1421, and he served as a scrupulously faithful supporter of the Albizzi. He was guilty of only one conspicuous act. He commissioned Filippo Brunelleschi, then at work on the dome of the cathedral, to design a sacristy for the church of San Lorenzo. But it was a pious act, for Giovanni no doubt did it in hopes that God, or at least the Pope, would then forgive him for usury.

In 1429 Giovanni died and left the leadership of his branch of the family to his son Cosimo—then a man of forty —who was cautious like his father, possessed of an iron will, incalculably clever—and very conspicuous indeed. When Cosimo died in 1464 at the age of seventy-five, the Florentines called him *Pater Patriae*, the father of their country.

Cosimo was the first of the eminent Florentine patrons of the arts. He pressed Brunelleschi to redesign the whole of San Lorenzo, and when the church was finished, it was the prime example of fifteenth-century Renaissance architecture in Florence. He built another, smaller church, La Badia, on the hills above Florence near Fiesole and commissioned Michelozzo Michelozzi to build a palace for the Medici in Florence. Here, Cosimo's caution showed: he had first asked Brunelleschi to design a palace, but when Brunelleschi's design seemed too grand, he had Michelozzo design a more modest one. He also had Michelozzo redesign the monastery of San Marco and its cloister (considered one of the finest in all Italy), and he commissioned Fra Angelico to decorate the prayer cells with his famous religious frescoes.

We shall hear more of Cosimo later as a patron of the arts and as a key figure in reviving the study of the ancient world—the revival from which the Renaissance, or "rebirth," takes its name. Suffice it to say for the moment that he was a most conspicuous figure in Florence. Lie as he might, he still had to report some income in 1457, and that report shows that he was at least four times wealthier than any other man in Florence. But he could afford to be wealthy

The pain and weariness of the aging, gout-ridden Cosimo de' Medici is captured in a medallion cast shortly after his death.

Cosimo was imprisoned in a cell behind the tiny window atop the Palazzo della Signoria—the government quarters later renamed Palazzo Vecchio, or "old palace."

and show it, for one of his first acts as head of the family was to get rid of the Albizzi and become the leading politician of Florence himself.

Just before the death of Giovanni, Rinaldo degli Albizzi had launched a war of conquest against the neighboring state of Lucca. As wars almost always do, this one spread, until Milan took the field against Florence as well. What it cost the Florentines to hire their batch of bungling mercenaries, and for Rinaldo himself to lead several disastrous campaigns, we cannot calculate certainly. It surely came close to ruining Florence utterly. Cosimo, like Giovanni, remained silent. He served loyally on the war board and waited. After the conflict had dragged on for four years, Rinaldo concluded an indifferent peace, and the Florentines were outraged. Never mind the cost or the moral questions; above all, Florentines never could bear to lose.

It was time, at last, for the Medici to make their move. Cosimo permitted word to leak out that he did not admire the way Rinaldo had handled the war, and that was sufficient. Having said only that much, in May of 1433 he transferred most of his money to his branch banks in Rome and Venice or stashed it in other more obscure places. He then left town for one of his country villas, for a rest.

By the end of the summer, Rinaldo realized that Cosimo's rumored remark had caused sentiment to build against the Albizzi government. On September 7 he summoned Cosimo to the government palace, the Palazzo Signoria, had him arrested, and locked him in a room high in the tower of the Palazzo. He then called for a parliament to vote on whether a *balìa* might be designated to reform the government.

In theory, a *balìa* was a committee authorized by an assembly of all citizens in the piazza in front of the Palazzo Signoria. The assembly was supposed to be a great democratic referendum—as the Greeks used to have in their ideal democratic city-states when all the people voted directly on an important issue. In practice, not all the citizens were admitted to the piazza. The streets were blocked off by the partisans of the government in power, and only loyal supporters were admitted to the piazza. They voted a clamorous "yes" to whatever was proposed, and the *balìa*—with this specific directive from the people—proceeded to "reform" the government. In this case, the reform consisted of exiling Cosimo and a number of his followers from Florence. It has been said that Cosimo escaped a sentence of death only by reaching one of the oligarchs with a handsome bribe.

Rinaldo should have murdered all the Medici. Cosimo's

The fourteenth-century rendering at right depicts an incident at Or San Michele, the great grain market of Florence, in a time of famine. Armed soldiers disperse the starving local people crowding about the empty grain bins.

trip to Venice, his appointed place of exile, was a prolonged triumphal parade. He was greeted in Venice like a king; he withdrew some funds from his bank there and paid to have the library at the monastery of San Giorgio rebuilt. Meanwhile, Rinaldo had not sufficiently "reformed" the government. One year later, in September, 1434, a pro-Medici government was elected. They, in their turn, called a parliament, and the *balìa* it selected reformed the government by exiling the Albizzi and bringing Cosimo back to Florence.

Cosimo's first move as the new political leader of Florence was to insure that he would never again be exiled. He accomplished this by a simple change in the electoral system. Before his time, the system of election worked like this: only members of the guilds were eligible for public office. All their names were thrown together and subjected to a "scrutiny"—that is, an examination to see who was qualified for office. The names of those qualified then were tossed into *borse*, or leather purses. At election time, which occurred every two months, the *borse* would be brought out, and the men whose names were drawn from these grab bags would serve in office. This election by pure chance was considered in most of Italy as the ultimate in fairness and democracy.

Obviously, only one thing was necessary to corrupt it. One needed only to control the scrutiny of names, make certain that only friends' names got in the *borse* to begin with—and one had a system controlled by bosses.

Alas, for Rinaldo degli Albizzi, it was not foolproof. For between the times when new names were picked for the *borse*, the people whose names were in the purse might change their minds. That is precisely what happened when Rinaldo was exiled and Cosimo returned to Florence. Cosimo's modification of the system was simplicity itself. He set up a committee of ten electors to draw names from the *borse*—by hand. The ten electors were the most strictly loyal followers of Cosimo, and they managed, therefore, to pick Medicean governments out of the *borse* for sixty years.

Cosimo was not a tyrant. But he certainly was what we would call today a political boss. Quiet, cautious, tight-lipped, he rarely appeared in public. He served only three two-month terms as Gonfalonier; that is, in thirty years of rule he was the official Florentine leader for six months.

His system of Medici control, while it never became a tyranny, became so secure that by Lorenzo's time no Florentine could have deluded himself to believe that he was not ruled by a monarch. Lorenzo was recognized as such throughout Europe. But the Florentines, declaiming as loudly as ever about their noble democracy, would not have traded him for a hundred honestly elected gonfaloniers.

A page from Lorenzo's son's arithmetic book (the Medici shield is at right). The wool trade was among the most important in Florence, and a mathematical problem is illustrated here by two merchants trading wool for cloth.

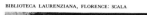

This fifteenth-century illustration from the record books of a merchant guild depicts an initiation ceremony—perhaps for a new guild member or for an officer.

Each of the three great Medici—Cosimo, his son Piero, and his grandson Lorenzo—suffered one attempt at rebellion, and each emerged from it stronger than before. In Cosimo's time, a group of citizens led by Luca Pitti thought that they would win popular favor, and the government, by campaigning to abolish the ten electors Cosimo had established. Cosimo permitted them to have their way, but after the electors had been abolished, the new government advocated a revision of the taxes. The plotters were undone. Revising the taxes would mean that they would have to pay more. They ran to Cosimo and begged him to call for a *balìa*. Only after several months did Cosimo permit a *balìa* to be formed. As a result, the electors were re-established, and Cosimo's control of the government was again confirmed.

In 1464 the seventy-five-year-old Cosimo went to his villa at Careggi to die. He offered advice to his son Piero, gave instructions for a plain funeral at San Lorenzo, and closed his eyes. When one of his family asked why he kept his eyes shut, he replied, "It is to accustom them to the dark."

He died of gout, that unglamorous illness that would also carry off Piero and Lorenzo. A rackingly painful disease that affects the joints and finally cripples, it is caused by an imbalance of uric acid in the system. That medical diagnosis would be mere esoterica were it not for the fact that uric acid is the chemical we now recognize as a stimulant to the brain. An excess of uric acid, then, causes gout—and often conspires to make brilliant men.

Cosimo was succeeded by his forty-eight-year-old son Piero, a man so afflicted with the family curse that he was known as Il Gottoso, "the gouty." He continued Cosimo's patronage of the arts and letters and no doubt would have counted among the finest of the Medici had he lived longer. He ruled a scant five years, and for the moment, all we need say of him is that once again a group of citizens led by the ever-ambitious Luca Pitti tried to seize control of the government, again by abolishing the ten electors.

This time Niccolò Soderini made all the speeches; the electors were abolished; and—remarkable coincidence!—Soderini himself was elected Gonfalonier. After a thoroughly undistinguished term, Soderini left office embittered and determined to get by force what he could not keep by favor. He and his fellow conspirators convinced Venice and several smaller states to send troops into Florence. At that moment, having borne all with patience, Piero acted decisively. He had been nursing his gout at Careggi but now came immediately to town, exposed the plot, called yet again for a *balìa*, and exiled the conspirators. Exiled them all, with the exception, that is, of Luca Pitti, who now begged for mercy. Piero gave him mercy of a sort and let him stay in Florence.

"You follow the infinite," Cosimo is alleged to have said to Luca one time, "and I the finite; you lay your ladders in the sky and I lean them close to earth lest I may fly so high that I may fear to fall." When Luca fell, he left his palace unfinished. He had begun it during Cosimo's reign, and when it was finished by others many years later, it was the most splendid palace in Florence. For the time being, however, the workmen refused to place a single stone for Luca, and the unfinished house stood for years as a monument to a foolish and vainglorious old man who died in abject humiliation—his blundering attempts to unseat the Medici serving only to place them more firmly in power.

In December of 1469 Piero succumbed to gout, and the mantle of power the Medici had woven so finely for themselves slipped easily onto the shoulders of the young Lorenzo, then at the end of his twentieth year. He had been tutored well to take his father's place. Three years before, his father had sent him on a tour of the diplomatic capitals of Italy and had written to him, at the end of his instructions, "in a word, it is necessary for thee now to be a man and not a boy."

On Piero's death, the leading citizens of the town gathered and offered control of the ruling party to Tommaso Soderini, the brother of the man prominent among the conspirators against Piero. Tommaso, however, was devoted to the Medici and insisted power should pass to Lorenzo. The leaders then went to Lorenzo and his sixteen-year-old brother, Giuliano. "Before the citizens departed," Machiavelli says, "they swore to regard the youths as their sons, and the brothers promised to look upon them as their parents."

Lorenzo himself recorded the event in his diary:

Although I, Lorenzo, was very young, being twenty years of age, the principal men of the city and of the state came to us in our house to condole with us on our loss and to encourage me to take charge of the city and of the state, as my grandfather and my father had done. This I did, though on account of my youth and the great responsibility and perils arising therefrom, with great reluctance, solely for the safety of our friends and of our possessions. For it is ill living in Florence for the rich unless they rule the state.

Mankind pays homage to the angel of Fame in a panel commissioned by the Medici at Lorenzo's birth.

26

II

MARKED FOR GREATNESS

The astrologers did not fail to note, when Lorenzo was born on January 1, 1449, that he was a Capricorn—endowed by the stars (so they must have reported to his father and grandfather) with strength, determination, and physical endurance. In truth, Lorenzo had more than that; as a child and young man, he had everything.

He was blessed with a strong, athletic body, intelligence, and a wide range of talents; he had all the money he could want, and he had a large, loving, and attentive family. To such a young man, nothing could seem impossible. He had the greatest asset any young man can have: he grew up believing that there were no limits to what he might achieve.

All of Lorenzo's natural abilities were developed to a point of excellence by the best education the Renaissance could provide. His education began, as does any child's, in his home, and his first lesson was the importance of the family itself. The primary source of power in Italy, Luigi Barzini has written, "is the family. The Italian family is a stronghold in a hostile land: within its walls and among its members, the individual finds consolation, help, advice, provisions, loans, weapons, allies and accomplices to aid him in his pursuits. . . . Scholars have always recognized the Italian family as the only fundamental institution in the country . . ."

The point cannot be overemphasized. All businesses in Italy were family businesses; all political parties, alliances of families—and alliances, domestic and foreign, were cemented by marriage.

The family extracts everybody's first loyalty [Barzini has written]. It must be defended, enriched, made powerful, respected, and feared by the use of whatever means are necessary. . . . Nobody should defy it with impunity. Its honor must not be tarnished. All wrongs done to it must be avenged. All enemies must be kept at bay and the dangerous ones deprived of power or destroyed. Every member is duty-bound to do all he can for its welfare, give his property if needed, and, sometimes, when it is absolutely inevitable, sacrifice his life. Men have spent their last penny to save a relative from bankruptcy.

Lorenzo learned all of this first, and he learned it well. The sanctity of the family explains many of his actions. Certainly, it helps explain the thoroughness with which the Pazzi family was punished: in the defense of his family, Lorenzo could be ferocious.

He learned everything of importance within the quiet and security of the massive stone walls of his own home. He learned first to recognize struggle and warfare as a familiar sight in Italy. On the wall of his own bedroom hung a huge painting by Paolo Uccello, *The Rout of San Romano* (see pages 48–49), a tumultuous tangle of lances and horses and armored soldiers that commemorates a victory by the Florentines over their neighboring town of Siena.

In the courtyard of his home was Donatello's statue of David—symbol of Florentine liberty. As the little David had conquered Goliath, so had Florence overcome the swaggering Duke of Milan in 1402. It was a lesson in courage and perseverance, of which Lorenzo was reminded daily by the presence of the statue.

Around the same courtyard were eight medallions by Donatello, copied from ancient cameos and medals, and from those, and from the books and manuscripts and other objects in his home, Lorenzo developed a curiosity and a knowledge of ancient Greece and Rome that he kept all his life.

In the small chapel of the Medici *palazzo* was Benozzo Gozzoli's gold-gilt fresco of the journey of the Magi, a constant reminder to Lorenzo that the kings of this world owe ultimate homage to God. It is said that the youngest of the three kings is the young Lorenzo himself—and if that is true, the painting must have had an especially strong impact on the young man. But the lesson would have been twofold: remember that you owe devotion to God; but remember, too, that you are a great prince of the world.

Cosimo had built country villas at Careggi, Fiesole, Trebbio, and Cafaggiolo outside Florence, and Lorenzo spent a good deal of time at them, learning to ride horses, to hunt, to bring down game birds with falcons—and learning, no doubt, how grapes are grown, how wines and cheeses are made, what the star constellations are, and a good bit else about the natural world that gave him a deep and abiding love of the country and of farming.

A masterpiece of early Renaissance art, Donatello's youthful David was acquired by the Medici for the courtyard of their palace.

Greek mythology was a frequent theme in Renaissance art. Here are two of the medallions depicting mythological scenes carved on the courtyard walls of the Medici Palace. At far left is the story of Athena and Poseidon; at left, the youthful Icarus dons his wings.

Surrounded by paintings and bronzes, sleeping in a great canopied bed, covered by gold-embroidered quilts, moving among tapestries, his touch always rewarded by the textures of velvets and silks, Lorenzo nonetheless avoided the greatest curse of the rich: he never was spoiled. He was born not to rest in his palace but to use it as a stronghold from which he could sally forth on new adventures and to which he always could return.

In addition to the lessons he simply absorbed from his surroundings, Lorenzo learned by example from his family. He was his father's and his grandfather's constant companion, and they made certain that he had the advantage of seeing the workings of the adult world at every opportunity. He watched as the very idea of capitalism took shape in the world, as many of the fundamental techniques of modern banking were worked out in his grandfather's study at the Palazzo Medici, and as his grandfather developed a new concept of business, what today would be called a conglomerate—a company with business interests in dozens of different enterprises.

Lorenzo watched as his father and grandfather received the resplendent ambassadors from Venice and France, the cardinals from Rome, and the slick politicians from the intriguing world of Florentine government—as his father and grandfather shrewdly dealt, cajoled, bargained, flattered, threatened, and perhaps, bribed their way through the thicket of business and politics. No doubt he was there to see his grandfather compose a letter to a foreign prince or give his instructions personally to an ambassador about to leave for Paris or to a bank manager about to leave for Bruges. He watched, he learned, and his father and grandfather tirelessly instructed him in all the knowledge and wiles that he one day would need as head of the Medici

OVERLEAF: *When Benozzo Gozzoli painted his fresco* Journey of the Magi *on the walls of the Medici chapel in 1459, he included likenesses of members of the family. Following the crowned figure, who might be Lorenzo, is Cosimo, riding a mule; to his left, astride a white horse, is Piero. Several rows back, between two bearded men, is the image of the artist, with his name on his cap.*

The fifteenth-century painting at left depicts the climax of a hunt—a moment that Lorenzo savoured often. The dogs have treed three fat birds, and the hunter, carrying his falcon, has just arrived on the scene. Realizing that most young boys would rather be off hunting than poring over textbooks, the illustrator of Lorenzo's son's arithmetic book enlivened his pages with vivid action scenes (right).

Piero probably was not naturally as brilliant as his father, yet he was reading the Latin poetry of Vergil at the age of six and writing letters to his father in Latin at the age of seven. Lorenzo's heart was in play.

He loved horses and hunting and athletics. It is said that his favorite horse would go days without eating if Lorenzo were not around to feed him. And Lorenzo already had begun to exhibit those characteristics that, while they probably horrified his mother, were to make him so popular as an adult: his dancing, his singing, his clowning, and his jokes. At Carnival time he was the life of the party; his gift for poetry turned into a talent for writing outlandishly bawdy songs, which he sang with unbounded enthusiasm, in a very bad singing voice, out of tune, and as loudly as he possibly could. For any excess energy, there was always a snowball fight, wrestling, tennis, and acrobatics. When he became older, he took out all this energy in great drinking bouts, hunting parties, and love affairs. He had, as one of his teachers generously put it, a "naturally joyful nature."

But then, had not Plato himself, in *The Republic*, advised young men to spend most of their time in athletics? He had indeed. "Gymnastics for the body," he had said, "and music for the soul." Gymnastics, he meant, to develop spir-

In one popular form of boxing (at right) the opponents stood on one another's feet and slugged away. Rules allowed ducking but forbade any change of stance. The riders in Florence's wild and dangerous horse races paid little heed to rules. In the fifteenth-century painting below, a large throng cheers the riders on to the finish.

itedness—and music and poetry and literature, later, to develop a refined restraint over the spiritedness.

Taking their cue from Plato, the Florentines pursued athletics with a vengeance at the playgrounds and the stadium beyond the town walls toward Pisa. It was there that they played a brutal game of football, called *palla al calcio*, with twenty-seven players on a team. It was there, among other places, that they boxed. (The style would have bewildered a modern boxer; one fighter would try to step on the other's feet, then, standing immobile, nose to nose, with bare fists, the two would beat each other to a pulp.) And it was from there that the horse races began. On the way from the stadium, down the stone streets and past the stone houses of Florence, to the finish line on the opposite side of town, riders were thrown onto the streets, spectators trampled, and horses terrified by fireworks. It was great fun.

Of Lorenzo as a teen-ager, we have only a few glimpses, but all the events we know of reveal that poise and self-assurance that seem to come naturally to an accomplished young athlete. When Luca Pitti tried to assassinate Lorenzo's father in 1466, when Lorenzo was seventeen, it was he, we are told, who saved his father's life.

The conspirators decided to murder Piero if they could not otherwise get hold of the government of the city, and they decided to waylay Piero as he was being carried (too crippled by the gout to ride) from a country villa to town. Lorenzo, however, had left the villa before his father, and so the story goes, when he came upon the armed men on the road, he kept them occupied, saying that his father would be along soon. Meanwhile, he sent a messenger back to tell his father to take a different road. The incident "gave a striking proof," one of Lorenzo's more grandiloquent biographers has said, "of that promptitude of mind which so eminently distinguished him on many subsequent occasions."

It was at this time, too, that Lorenzo's father sent him on his diplomatic tour of Pisa, Milan, Venice, Bologna, and Ferrara. Diplomacy being, by nature, a secretive business, we do not know just what Lorenzo was meant to accom-

Mino da Fiesole was one of the first Renaissance sculptors to depict his subjects as he saw them—without flattery or idealization. His bold, candid bust of Lorenzo's father, Piero, dates from 1453.

MUSEO NAZIONALE, FLORENCE

38

plish. Probably he was required only to be agreeable and meet the leaders with whom he one day would have to deal.

In any event, he was adjudged such a success on his tour that his father immediately dispatched him to Rome to see the Pope. Several Italian states were—typically—stirring up trouble and threatening general war. Lorenzo's job was to keep the Pope from joining in the hostilities. It was an easy job, but an important one, and it is apparent that Lorenzo's gout-ridden father already had come to rely heavily on his son, for advice as well as mere diplomatic travel, before Lorenzo's eighteenth birthday. In Lorenzo's absence, Piero wrote, he was "as a man without hands."

It is very much in character that Lorenzo's first big splash as a young man was made on horseback. He competed in a jousting tournament, the Renaissance counterpart of the modern football game or track meet, in the piazza in front of the church of Santa Croce. The tourney was arranged for February 7, 1469, and it was intended to celebrate his wedding, the following June, to a young red-headed Roman girl named Clarice Orsini.

The tourney was a major event in Florence, and preceding it, there was a procession of the competitors into the piazza, led by nine trumpeters, three pages, two squires in full armor, twelve mounted noblemen, and then Lorenzo's brother, Giuliano. Giuliano wore a tabard of silver brocade, a "silk doublet . . . embroidered in pearls and silver. His black velvet cap was adorned with three feathers worked in gold thread, and set in pearls and rubies." Then there were five more pages on horseback, a line of fifers and drummers —and finally, Lorenzo himself.

He came, mounted on a horse presented by [King] Ferrante of Naples, richly caparisoned in red and white velvet adorned with pearls. Lorenzo wore a surcoat with puffings of red and white silk at the shoulders, and over the surcoat a broad silk scarf embroidered with roses, some fresh, some withered, with the motto, "Le Temps Revient" [Time Returns], picked out upon the scarf in pearls. His black velvet cap was studded with pearls, and from it there sprang a feather of gold thread, spangled with rubies and diamonds. . . . His shield had for its centerpiece the great Medici diamond, "Il Libro," estimated to be worth two thousand fiorini. . . .

It goes on and on, this description of pomp, with ten mounted cavaliers, sixty-four footmen, and so forth. Nobody outdid the Florentines in their love of a good parade.

With the motto "Le Temps Revient," Lorenzo announced, with brash immodesty, his ideal for Florence. The

Florentine knights—their names emblazoned on their reins—compete in a tournament in the Piazza Santa Croce. Elegant ladies and gentlemen and a group of red-robed merchants have good balcony seats, while many young men and children peer through knotholes and cheer from crude platforms.

words are, as Vincent Cronin has written:

a translation into the language of chivalry of Dante's "secol si rinova," in turn a paraphrase of Vergil's fourth eclogue. In that poem, written about forty years before Christ, Vergil foretells the birth of a miraculous baby, which would mark the opening of a new age of the world, a golden age corresponding to the idyllic first beginnings, where there would be no more suffering or

bloodshed. The child when grown was to become a god and rule the world in perfect peace. By evoking this, Lorenzo was pledging himself to give Florence a golden age free from war, and therefore amenable to intellectual and artistic pursuits.

In the jousting, Lorenzo took on four challengers and defeated them all. His friend the poet Luigi Pulci was moved to compare him to Achilles. Lorenzo was more mod-

Lorenzo's wife, Clarice, appears as a somber and rather uninterested attendant in Ghirlandaio's late-fifteenth-century painting entitled The Birth of the Virgin.

est; he knew he was given first prize more for his position than for his performance, and self-deception was not one of his faults: "Although I was not a very vigorous warrior, nor a hard hitter, the first prize was adjudged to me, a helmet inlaid with silver and a figure of Mars as the crest."

Given to celebrate his forthcoming marriage, the tournament was, in fact, presented in honor of Lorenzo's mistress Lucrezia Donati, a lovely young Florentine girl whom Lorenzo loved passionately, and to whom he wrote a number of sonnets. A descendant of Gemma Donati, who had been Dante's wife, she was, in Lorenzo's words, "astonishing. She was of a just and proper height. . . . Her countenance was serious without being severe; mild and pleasant, without levity or vulgarity. Her eyes were lively, without any indication of pride or conceit. . . . In walking, in dancing, or in other exercises which display the person, every motion was elegant and appropriate. . . . there was nothing which could be desired in a beautiful and accomplished woman, which was not in her most abundantly found. . . ."

Apparently, few people were shocked by Lorenzo's state of affairs, that he should love Lucrezia and marry Clarice, that he should celebrate his wedding with a tourney—given in honor of his mistress. Lucrezia Donati was of too modest a family for Lorenzo to marry. His marriage instead to Clarice Orsini was recognized as a simple diplomatic maneuver. Lorenzo was not expected to love his wife—and he never did. He respected her, was affectionate toward her, had several children by her; but he reserved his passion for his mistresses.

Love and marriage were not thought necessarily to go together. In rare instances when they did, so much the better. But the purpose of marriage during the Renaissance was the strengthening of the family through good alliances.

Clarice was by no means beautiful, and she must have been an aggravating young woman, too pious for Lorenzo's tastes, uncomfortable in the easygoing, boisterous, and intellectually brilliant Medici entourage, rigid and old-fashioned in the rearing of her children. It is interesting to observe that their only serious difficulty arose over the education of their children.

Lorenzo hired his friend, the leading poet of the day, Angelo Poliziano, to tutor the children. Angelo schooled them in Latin and Greek by having them read the ancient "pagan" poets of Greece and Rome. Clarice wanted him to have the children learn their Latin from the writings of the Fathers of the Church. When Angelo scheduled a Greek les-

Sedate wedding guests dance beneath a gay canopy in this painting from a fifteenth-century marriage chest.

son, Clarice took the children off to sing psalms. Lorenzo finally solved the problem by moving his friend to another of his country villas, but the children learned of the "pagan" writers anyway from other tutors.

They were married on Sunday, June 4, 1469, and the celebration matched the splendor of the tourney four months earlier. There were five banquets in three days, at which one hundred fifty calves and two thousand brace of capons were consumed along with oceans of wine and other comestibles. Clarice wore a gown of gold and white brocade and rode a horse from the royal Neapolitan stables. Fifty young dancing girls sat at her table, while hundreds of elder citizens, Florence's leading businessmen and aristocrats, were deployed at several other tables.

In this fifteenth-century manuscript illustration one tailor works on a piece of cloth while another fits a fashionable young rake in a suit of the latest style.

The Medici home that day was a carnival of silks and satins, Oriental rugs, velvets and ermines, all of it lit with thousands of wax candles; and the company was entertained with dances and music and songs, some of the songs written, no doubt, by Lorenzo himself. Some years later Lorenzo recorded the spectacular event in his memoirs: "I, Lorenzo, took for wife Clarice, daughter of the lord Jacopo," he wrote coolly and tersely, "or rather she was given to me."

Six months later, his father died, and Lorenzo became the first citizen of Florence. His training held him in good stead until 1471, when he made one of the bitterest blunders of his life, involving both business and politics.

As the economy of Florence was based upon textiles, the mineral alum was indispensable to the Florentine wool merchants. Alum was used to fix the dyes in woolen cloth— and it was the brilliant colors of Florentine cloth that made it prized throughout the world. The Medici conglomerate had a virtual monopoly on alum in Europe. When deposits of the mineral were discovered in the papal state of Tolfa in 1468, the Medici were given management of the mines. When another deposit was discovered in Ischia, the Medici arranged an agreement with its owner to insure continued control of the market. Then, in 1471, an alum deposit was discovered near Volterra, a small town that owed its allegiance to Florence.

It later turned out that the Volterran deposits were not worth mining, but for the moment they seemed to promise a fortune. A Florentine company drew up a contract for the alum with the town government of Volterra. The Volterrans, learning of it, felt that they had been sold cheaply by their government. First they demonstrated, and the town in turn closed the mines until a new contract could be negotiated. Florence, acting in its turn to protect the interests of its company, ordered the Volterrans to open the mines again. The Volterrans responded by rising up in a violent riot in which two of the company's shareholders were killed.

Lorenzo had been at the helm in Florence for two years when this imbroglio presented itself to him. But his position was complicated. Tommaso Soderini had arranged the smooth transition from Piero to Lorenzo, and Lorenzo and Giuliano had promised to look upon Soderini and the other leaders "as their parents." In short, Lorenzo did not yet feel as though he, and he alone, led Florence.

When Volterra revolted, Soderini promptly advised Lorenzo to let the Volterrans have their way. But Lorenzo,

This brightly glazed terra-cotta emblem belonged to the important Florentine wool merchants' guild.

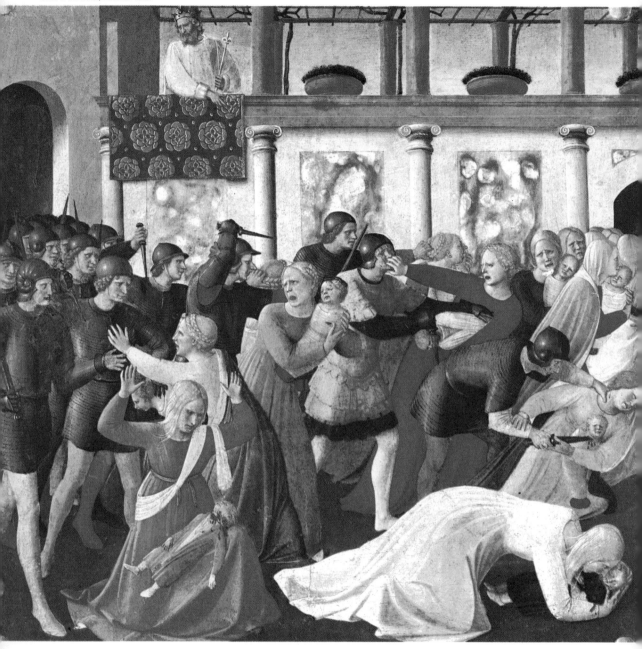

Fra Angelico's fresco depicting the biblical story of King Herod's slaughter of the Innocents is symbolic in setting and costume of the atrocities committed against civilians during the power struggles in Renaissance Italy. One such atrocity was the sacking of the town of Volterra by Lorenzo's mercenary troops in 1471.

as Machiavelli wrote, "thinking this an opportunity for exhibiting his prudence and wisdom, and being strenuously supported by those who envied the influence of Tommaso Soderini, resolved to march against [Volterra], and punish the arrogance of the people of Volterra with arms, declaring that if [the Volterrans] were not made a striking example, others would, without the least fear or respect, upon every slight occasion, adopt a similar course."

Pity the poor Volterrans. They knew that they were treading on dangerous ground in tangling with Florence. But they did not know that Lorenzo was impatient to make his own move, to show that he, and he alone, held the reins of government in Florence.

Again, Machiavelli reports: "The Florentines . . . assembled ten thousand foot and two thousand horse, who, under the command of Federigo, lord of Urbino, marched into the country of Volterra and . . . encamped before the city." The Volterrans soon capitulated, but then came the tragedy. The soldiers, as was the habit with mercenaries, got out of the control of their leader and marched into the town to destroy and loot it, "neither women nor sacred places being spared; and the soldiery . . . plundered all that came within their reach."

The Florentines actually rejoiced over the event; none of their small, subject towns, they felt, should be permitted to defy Florence with impunity, and Lorenzo was celebrated as a heroic, forceful leader.

But Lorenzo never ceased to regret the fact that he had set going what became a punitive expedition against a traditionally friendly town, and the memory of the sacking of Volterra haunted him the rest of his life. In terms of simple, realistic politics, too, he probably came to agree with Soderini. Asked afterward what he thought of the victory, Soderini said, "To me the place seems rather lost than won; for had it been received on equitable terms, advantage and security would have been the result; but having to retain it by force, it will in critical junctures occasion weakness and anxiety, and in times of peace, injury and expense."

For all the mixed feelings about the Volterran revolt, the event marked, nonetheless, the real beginning of Lorenzo's leadership of Florence. He had made the decision. He had commanded an army to take the field. He had been —and this, above all, must have been noted by the other leaders of Italy—thoroughly tough and uncompromising.

And of course, it marked the end of Lorenzo's youth. For now he had blood on his hands.

III

WAR OVER THE BALANCE OF

POWER

In his essay *On Poetics*, Aristotle defined the "perfect plot" for a drama as having a "change in the hero's fortunes . . . from happiness to misery; and the cause of it must lie . . . in some great error on his part." It was essential, in Aristotle's view, that the greatest characters in a play have a "tragic flaw"—a fault in their characters that causes their downfall. In this neat, classical sense, Lorenzo de' Medici may be said to have had a tragic flaw: impulsiveness.

Impulsiveness is what made Lorenzo an appealing man. It was the trait that led him to be spontaneous and ener-

In the mid-fifteenth century Piero de' Medici commissioned this painting by Paolo Uccello for the Medici palace. Entitled Rout of San Romano, *it is one of three large panels celebrating the pageantry of Renaissance warfare as Uccello imagined it. Another panel hung in Lorenzo's bedroom.*

49

getic, to take up sudden friendships and interests, to do the myriad things he did to inspire Renaissance Florence. It also was the trait that led him to the sacking of Volterra—and that led him irretrievably into the Pazzi assassination and war in 1478.

When the Pazzi killed Giuliano that Sunday morning—in the attempted coup described earlier by Machiavelli and the shopkeeper Luca Landucci—they did not do so without provocation. Indeed, there had been a long and complicated background of rivalries and struggles—a background that we now must go back to in order to understand the events of that Sunday and of the years that followed.

The Pazzi were an old and highly respected Florentine family. They were, in fact, allies of the Medici, well within the circles of power, and their alliance had been duly solemnized by the marriage of Lorenzo's childhood friend Guglielmo Pazzi to Lorenzo's sister Bianca.

At the same time, however, the Pazzi and the Medici were business rivals. Like the Medici, the Pazzi had risen to wealth in the late fourteenth century. By the early 1470's, after the revolt at Volterra, the Rome branch of the Pazzi bank, under the management of Francesco de' Pazzi, was one of the foremost competitors of the Medici bank. Francesco, a short, thin, restless dandy, was the very stuff of which jealous conspirators are made. He spent hours every day with the barber, having his unusually light-colored hair fussed over, and in manners and dress he was the very picture of a prancing, conceited, self-important bachelor. A passionately ambitious young hothead, he burned to take the lucrative papal bank account away from the Medici.

But if Francesco and his family were ambitious, they were mere novices of ambition compared to Pope Sixtus IV, the man who "elevated nepotism into political principle." He was born of a humble family and educated by Franciscan monks. A small, rotund man, with cold, unflinching eyes and a nose pinched into a permanent sneer, Sixtus had fought his way up through the Franciscan order and managed election to the papacy when one of his nephews bargained like an unscrupulous politician—promising ecclesiastical promotions in exchange for votes for his uncle. With one hand Sixtus built the beautiful Sistine Chapel and added to the Vatican Library, and with the other he wielded a sword, like any grasping Italian prince, to conquer territory in Italy to give to his family. When one thinks of the corruption of the papacy that helped

Proud and ambitious, the Pazzi family—archenemy of the Medici —lived sumptuously, and like other aristocratic families of the day, were eager patrons of the arts. Commissioned by the Pazzi in the fifteenth century, this serene, dignified chapel was designed in the classical style of ancient Rome.

bring on the Protestant Reformation fifty years later, one thinks first of Sixtus, rich, arrogant, incomparably ambitious. And harsh: it was Sixtus who instituted the Spanish Inquisition.

Four months after he had bargained himself into the papacy, Sixtus made cardinals of two of his nephews and bestowed pieces of the Italian countryside on them on a grand and lavish scale. One of them went on a buying spree—horses and gold and carpets and tapestries and mistresses and food and drink—and died in 1474 after a breathtaking two years of high living. Sixtus promptly made room for two more of his nephews, one of them Girolamo Riario. Girolamo, like several other of the Pope's nephews, was widely thought to be Sixtus' bastard son—a not surprising assumption, since bastard sons were commonplace in the Vatican during the Renaissance. In Girolamo's case, however, the rumor was slanderous; he was the legitimate son of Sixtus' sister. A prissy-lipped young nitwit with vacuous eyes, Girolamo had a blind, clumsy ambition that approached the magnitude of Sixtus' own.

GABRIELIS·ZERBI·VERONENSIS· IN·QVAESTIONIBVS·METAPHY SICIS·QVAS·EDIDIT·PROLOGVS·

Rerum maxime scibiliū speculatio q̃ multitudis vsus metaphice nūcupat. Sapientissimus vo Aristoteles theologiā. primam phīam. ꝗ sapientiaz. inter oia hūana studia psectioz est. ꝗ sblimioz. vtilioz. ꝗ iucundioz. ¶Perfectioz quidē. nam cū bene viuere seu vita cum virtute ꝗ felicitas oiuz sint eligibilissima. viŋ°. politicoz. licet adipiscendi hec aliquibus insit potestas: alijs vero nō ꝗpter fortunam quādam aut naturam. quātum homo sapiētie studio incubuerit tantuz felicitatis ad quaz est eius naturale desideriuz adi

piscetur. Propter quod recte inqt phus. vi. ethicoz. sapiens maxime erit felix. ¶Sublimioz aūt est eo q̃ metaphica speculatio itellectū hominis pficit magis hm q̃ diuinum quoddam. cum ipsa nō sit intellectus nostri in eo q̃ est humanus. sed in eo pro vt diuinū quoddam in nobis existit. Plurime nāqꝝ cum sint hominis in eo q̃ homo ꝓprietates vt verecūdari de turpi perpetrato. discernere inter honestum ꝗ in honestū. habere amiciciam hm omne genus amicicie itellectualibus theoromatibus ꝗ speculari ꝗ delectari delectatione ꝝtrariuz nō habente. ꝗ similes ¶Precipua tamen hominis ꝓprietas in eo q̃ est quoddam diuinum ut testatur Hermes trimegistus de deo deoꝝ ad Esclipium collegam est. q̃ solus homo nexus est dei ꝗ mūdi

A i

Although the Italian Renaissance often is associated with a rise of secularism in Christian civilization, the papacy scarcely was diminished in influence. The Pope remained a powerful leader, as likely to partake of as to resist the growth of scholarship in nontheological areas. Fascinated by the Classical studies of his contemporaries, Pope Sixtus IV stocked the Vatican Library with manuscripts. A page from one, Questiones Metaphysicae *(opposite), shows the Pontiff accepting the treatise from the author, Gabrielle Zerbi. Above is Sixtus' papal ring and at right the golden rose of the papacy, made by a Florentine craftsman and presented to the town of Siena by the Pope. In 1473 Sixtus built the Sistine Chapel at the Vatican; the structure achieved its greatest fame after 1508, when Pope Julius ordered Michelangelo to begin his magnificent murals on the ceiling. The subject of the series is* The Creation; *the segment below illustrates the temptation of Eve by the serpent of Eden.*

To Riario, Sixtus promised nothing less than an entire state, which he intended to carve out of the lovely alpine countryside northeast of Florence, in the Romagna.

Unfortunately for the peace of Italy, the Romagna sprawled directly across the trade route between Florence and Venice. In effect, then, Riario's state would cut Florence off from the Adriatic Sea and from Venice—and go far toward surrounding and isolating the Florentines.

In 1473, therefore, moving to protect his access to the Adriatic, Lorenzo decided to slice the new state in half by purchasing the town of Imola from his ally the Duke of Milan. The Duke first agreed to sell Imola to Lorenzo, then, seeing the chance of a larger profit, decided to bargain Lorenzo off against the Pope. In the end, the Duke betrayed Lorenzo and agreed to sell Imola to Sixtus for forty thousand ducats.

Coolly, Sixtus turned to the Medici bank and asked for a loan of forty thousand ducats. Lorenzo delayed, and Sixtus then shifted to Francesco de' Pazzi and plopped the ripe papal account into his lap. Sixtus got the forty thousand ducats from his willing new banker and closed the deal to buy Imola.

With one stroke, Lorenzo had been put into an intolerable position. His pride injured, his maneuver in the Romagna thwarted, his trade route choked off—and certainly not least—a branch of his bank lopped off disdainfully: it was too much to bear. Given the characters of the Pazzi, the Pope, and Lorenzo, the steps leading to the impasse seem to have been inevitable. Then Lorenzo added the last touch that forced the conflicting ambitions into open war: his own impulsiveness.

He had Florence's governing council summon Francesco de' Pazzi from his Rome bank to Florence. Francesco arrived in Florence cheerfully, expecting nothing, and he was given a slap in the face and a rap in his pocketbook. A retroactive law regarding intestacy had been passed. Never mind what the law stated. It was drafted in the most bewildering language possible—in order to hide its intent. Its intent, however, was crystal-clear: the Pazzi family had inherited money, by virtue of the marriage of one of the Pazzi sons to the rich daughter of a Borromeo. The retroactive

Amid the ornate surroundings of a Vatican chamber, Sixtus IV is pictured by Melozzo da Forli as the Pontiff receives a new director for his pet project, the Vatican Library. With Sixtus are the four nephews on whom he showered so many riches; one (center) would become Pope Julius II.

TEMPLA DOMVM EXPOSITIS:VICOS FORA MOENIA PONTES:
VIRGINEAM TRIVII QVOD REPARARIS AQVAM:
PRISCA LICET NAVTIS STATVAS DARE COMMODA PORTVS:
ET VATICANVM CINGERE SIXTE IVGVM:
PLVS TAMEN VRBS DEBET: NAM QVAE SQVALORE LATEBAT:
CERNITVR IN CELEBRI BIBLIOTHECA LOCO.

In this primitive fifteenth-century chronicle illustration, the stubble-bearded King Ferrante—who was a leader of the forces opposing Lorenzo—rides in procession.

law now changed that, snatched the money from the Pazzi family, and bestowed it on another relative, who, as it happened, was a friend of the Medici. It was robbery without a doubt, and Francesco recognized it instantly as a robbery of revenge. That, he was told in effect, would teach him to cross Lorenzo.

It was Lorenzo's brother, Giuliano, who later paid with his life for these increasing hostilities; yet ironically, it was Giuliano who now told the quick-tempered Lorenzo that he was being too severe. He recognized that Lorenzo was not simply retaliating against Francesco for the loan to Sixtus, but that Lorenzo, in total exasperation, had decided to reduce the power of the Pazzi family altogether and eliminate them as serious rivals. According to Machiavelli, Giuliano "often complained to his brother Lorenzo of the affair, saying he was afraid that by grasping at too much they would lose all. Lorenzo, flushed with youth and power, would assume the direction of everything, and resolved that all transactions should bear an impress of his influence."

Lorenzo surely could have found a way to temper the affair, had he been patient enough to work for some acceptable, cordial relationship with the Pazzi. He was not. He was aching for a fight.

The animosities deepened quickly—and the moves and countermoves became so confusing that not even the disputants were certain of who had done what and whether or not they had meant it. Lorenzo gave aid to an adventurer named Niccolò Vitelli when he led the papal town of Città di Castello in a revolt against Sixtus. In return, Sixtus disregarded Florence's wishes (which he usually honored) in appointing an archbishop for the neighboring town of Pisa; in 1475 he tried to force upon the Florentines his cohort Francesco Salviati. The newly appointed Archbishop of Pisa was one of those essentially cowardly men who are always dangerous. Living in timid fear, too weak to act with purpose and manliness, they strike out viciously when cornered. With the mere threat of armed intervention, Lorenzo frightened Salviati from Pisa and kept him for three years from taking his post. Elsewhere, and suddenly, a *condottiere*, or soldier of fortune, named Carlo Fortebraccio attempted to seize the town of Perugia in 1477, and the Pope—suspicious now of all ill fortune that befell him, and prepared to blame everything on Lorenzo—accused Lorenzo of aiding Fortebraccio.

Frustrated at every turn, Sixtus came to believe that all the opposition to him was being artfully arranged in Florence. Therefore, slowly and carefully, he set about to tip the delicate balance of power in Italy by robbing Florence of her strongest ally, King Ferrante of Naples.

Jacob Burckhardt, the famous nineteenth-century historian of the Renaissance, wrote a description of King Ferrante that the Florentines would have recognized:

It is certain that he was equaled in ferocity by none among the princes of his time. Restlessly active, recognized as one of the most powerful political minds of the day, . . . he concentrated all his powers, among which must be reckoned profound dissimulation and an irreconcilable spirit of vengeance, on the destruction of his opponents. . . . Extreme measures became part of his daily policy. . . . Besides hunting . . . his pleasures were of two kinds: he liked to have his opponents near him, either alive in well-guarded prisons, or dead and embalmed, dressed in the costume which they wore in their lifetime.

Generously plying Ferrante with favors, Sixtus gradually won him over. Lorenzo, for his part, had added Venice to his existing alliance with Milan. Thus, by 1478, the two southern powers came to be arrayed against the three northern powers of Italy. The outbreak of war awaited only the entry upon the scene of someone impatient for change. That someone was the Pope's insatiable nephew Girolamo Riario, now installed in the town of Imola and anxious to enlarge his domain to the scale his uncle had promised.

Riario took it upon himself to seek out the most likely men to join a conspiracy against Lorenzo. He recruited Francesco de' Pazzi and the nervously angry Archbishop Salviati, and the three of them went to the Pope with the proposal that they get rid of Lorenzo. Thus were the forces assembled for assassination on that fateful Sunday in 1478.

Historians always have maintained that the Pope agreed to the plan of the conspirators but that he insisted that there be "no bloodshed." But to imagine that Sixtus could be innocent enough, in that time of extravagantly generous bloodshed, to believe that Lorenzo could be removed without murder is to imagine far too much.

In fact, when the Pope heard the news of the assassina-

In 1478 Pope Sixtus IV excommunicated Lorenzo and denied benefit of the clergy to the Florentines, who imagined themselves destined for the Purgatory and Hell described by Dante in The Divine Comedy. *Domenico de Michelino's painting pictures the horror, with Dante as narrator.*

tion attempt in the cathedral, he was dismayed—but his dismay was over the fact that Lorenzo, too, had not been killed, that the government had not been wrested from the Medici. In short, the Pope repented—that the plan had failed. He first launched a war of bitter invective against Lorenzo and ordered that the Medici property in Rome be confiscated. Then he directed that all Florentines in Rome were to be jailed. And finally he insisted that Lorenzo come to Rome to make amends for the mob having hanged Archbishop Salviati after the assassination. When Lorenzo ignored his demand, the Pope excommunicated Lorenzo and all the public officials of Florence. The papal bull of excommunication referred modestly to the gentleness and patience of the Pope's own character and styled Lorenzo as "the child of iniquity and the nursling of perdition."

Ultimately, all Florence was denied benefit of clergy. In our own godless age, it may be difficult to understand the devastation that the Florentines felt at this change of fortune. They felt, in short, that they ran the risk of going to Hell by defying the Pope, and they knew precisely what Hell would be from Dante's *Inferno* and from the countless pictures and sermons that told them about it: an eternity of fire and brimstone, of gnashing of teeth, of incredible and unspeakable suffering.

Lorenzo, declaring that the wrath of the Pope was directed principally against himself, offered himself up as the sacrificial lamb. He would, he said, surrender himself to the Pope if the Florentines wished him to do so. In the classic Aristotelian sense, by his own mistakes, Lorenzo had gone from happiness to misery and all that was needed was a chorus of Florentine women to come on stage to speak the moral and mark the end of "The Tragedy of Lorenzo."

In a most un-Aristotelian turn of events, Lorenzo was given a second chance. The Florentines refused to accept his sacrifice. Next, the Pope demanded that Florence surrender Lorenzo or else prepare for war. And with that, the Pope had made a terrible blunder. Whatever else the Florentines might bow to, they never would tolerate a threat, and they answered the Pope's demand with undisguised scorn. War thus was declared, and in July of 1478 the combined forces of Sixtus and King Ferrante of Naples moved into the southern end of the Chiana valley, some fifty-five miles south of Florence.

The Chiana valley, a broad, marshy savanna forty miles long and twenty-five miles wide, was the sole large piece of territory in the area where it was easy to move an army. The rest of the landscape was replete with heavily battlemented towns bristling among mountain peaks. Whatever route the enemy took, therefore, it was bound to be a circuitous valley path around impassable mountains, with the constant threat of harassment from the towns.

Now two more characters enter the drama: Alfonso, Duke of Calabria, and Federigo da Montefeltro, Duke of Urbino—the leaders of the Papal-Neapolitan armies. Alfonso, the son of King Ferrante of Naples, was described by Burckhardt as "a savage, brutal profligate" and by another historian as "the cruelest, worst, most vicious, and basest man ever seen." Worse than Sixtus, than Francesco de' Pazzi, and Girolamo Riario? It seems hard to believe. In any case, clearly another villain had come upon the stage.

It is a pleasure to report, however, that Federigo da Montefeltro was a good man. True enough, he made his living from war; he was a professional soldier and hired out to the highest bidder. But again to quote Burckhardt:

Feeling secure in [his own state of Urbino] where all gained profit or employment from his rule, and where none were beggars, he habitually went unarmed and almost unaccompanied; alone among the princes of his time he ventured to walk in an open park, and to take his frugal meals in an open chamber, while Livy, or in time of fasting some devotional work, was read to him. In the course of the same afternoon he would listen to a lecture on some classical subject, and thence would go to the monastery of the Clarisse and talk of sacred things through the grating with the abbess.

He was a distinguished patron of the arts, an excellent administrator, much admired by the people he ruled—in many ways a match for the magnificent Lorenzo. That he had lost his right eye in a jousting tourney lent a little panache to his hawk-nosed visage, even though it was an embarrassment to him: after the loss, he always turned his left profile to artists when he posed for a portrait.

On July 11 Alfonso and Federigo crossed the Florentine frontier near the mountain bastion of Montepulciano. Then, abruptly, they wheeled to their left, seized Castellina and Radda, and headed west for the Elsa valley and the Florentine fortress of Poggio Imperiale.

Sitting erect, a piece of armor beside him symbolizing his prowess at war, his left profile carefully turned to hide his missing right eye, the Duke of Urbino—allied with Ferrante against Lorenzo—sits with his young son.

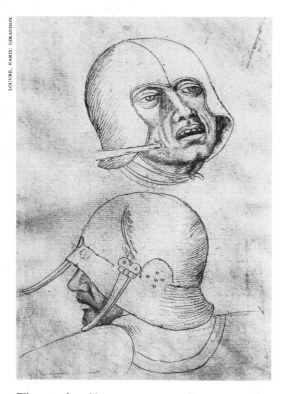

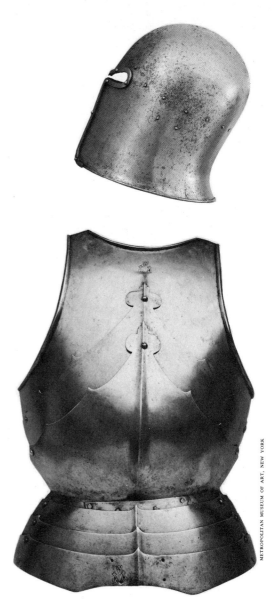

The art of making armor was an important profession in fifteenth-century Italy; and the Missaglia family of Milan—who made the breastplate and helmet at right—were Italy's leading armorers. But as the drawings above show, the helmets worn by Lorenzo's mercenaries did not afford complete protection.

The Florentines waited, and waited, and waited—not because they had a brilliant counterstrategy and wished to lead the enemy into a trap, but because the astrologers had told them that the propitious moment for attack would not come until 10:30 on the morning of September 27—and still, in that enlightened age, the Florentines were not yet prepared to throw over all their old, reliable medieval superstitions. On September 27 the Florentine war commission gave the *bâton* of command, as Edward Armstrong has written, "to the most incompetent of generals," Ercole d'Este, Duke of Ferrara.

After all these elaborate preparations, the venting of real passions, and real murders in real cathedrals, the war itself must come as something of an anticlimax. Even before Ercole d'Este took the field, Alfonso and Federigo looked over the fortress of Poggio Imperiale and decided that it was depressingly difficult to attack. Instead of laying siege to Poggio, they turned around, marched all the way back to the Chiana valley, and laid siege to the town of San Savino. D'Este, urged by the Florentines to take up the chase, camped instead at a safe distance from the enemy and did not finally move against them until it was too late. San Savino, key to the Ambra valley and thus to the Arno valley, had fallen.

All that saved Florence—the astrologers could have predicted it—was the inclination of the axis of the planet earth; that is, November had come, and the troops called the customary winter truce and retired to their quarters. The first year of the war was ended.

In the spring of 1479 this desultory war would become more exciting, but some word must be said immediately about the appalling fact that, so far in the war, there was no meeting between the two armies. Not a single captain had been killed, nor would a soldier of that rank be killed in the entire war. As Luca Landucci wrote in his diary in August, 1478, "The rule for our Italian soldiers seems to be this: 'You pillage there, and we will pillage here; there is no need for us to approach too close to one another.'"

Warfare in Renaissance Italy was a strange phenomenon. First, it was fought not by citizen armies but by mercenaries—men who fought for pay and were interested only in pay. They were free-lance soldiers and would fight for anyone who would finance them. Duke Federigo, now in the employ of the Pope, was the man who had led his forces into Volterra for Lorenzo a few years earlier. Had the soldiers been loyal to one side or the other, no doubt they would have fought with greater determination. Paid for the time they put in, they were interested in prolonging the war for as long a time as possible.

Then, too, the mercenary leaders had marriage alliances no less than other Italian leaders. Ercole d'Este had not been too anxious to defend San Savino for more reasons than his innate mercenary caution: the attacker, King Ferrante's son Alfonso, was Ercole's brother-in-law.

Because they wished to prolong the war, and because they were not anxious to kill their enemies, and last but not least, because Renaissance towns were so difficult to

This fifteenth-century version of King Minos' retreat after his unsuccessful
siege of Athens reveals the reason why most generals tried to avoid a direct

invasion of a walled Renaissance city. Whenever possible, a siege was used as a blockade, with the attacker hoping to starve the town into submission.

attack by virtue of their stone walls and usually commanding hilltop positions, warfare consisted primarily of protracted sieges. An army would camp around a town and wait for the inhabitants to run out of food. When food ran out, the town would surrender, the army would secure it, and then another town would be laid under siege. Open, pitched battles between armies were avoided at all costs. A first-rate general might fight an entire war without ever getting his men into a battle.

Only one factor kept this sort of warfare from being a completely enjoyable way to knock about the countryside for a few months. Mercenaries lived on what they could steal as well as on what they were paid, and when supplies were low, they lived off the produce of the land, too. The destruction of crops led to famine. Famine led inexorably to its twin horror, plague, and plague cast a pall over Renaissance warfare that made it thoroughly miserable. No Italian had forgotten the Black Death of the 1340's, when the population of Florence was reduced by one half and that of Siena dropped from forty-five thousand to a shattered fifteen thousand. The prospect of plague was quite as terrifying as the threat today of nuclear destruction—and much more within the realm of expectation. Warfare, then, was a matter of attrition and exhaustion, the question being who first would run out of money to pay their mercenaries or first succumb to starvation and plague.

In the spring of 1479 the Florentine troops came out of winter quarters with renewed spirits. In a dashing flanking maneuver, they threatened the capture of Perugia. When enemy forces went to meet them there, Florentine forces up at Poggio Imperiale worried the enemy's other flank, driving down toward Siena as far as Casole.

The war should have turned in Florence's favor, but alas, the victory over Casole led to Florence's defeat. The mercenaries, as it turned out, flushed with their conquest, began to fight among themselves over the spoils. "It was thought," Machiavelli reports, "that if they remained long in company, they would turn their arms against each other." Reluctant to take up arms against the enemy, the mercenaries were well prepared to battle among themselves over booty. They had to be separated, and this division in the ranks seriously weakened the Florentine position in the

Within view of the city they are preparing to invade, the soldiers in this sixteenth-century woodcut maneuver for the imminent battle.

The fifteenth-century manuscript illustration opposite depicts the gloom of a plague-stricken town. Most of the houses are shuttered and deserted; only a courageous physician remains to care for the sick and dying victims.

Elsa valley. Sensing their opportunity, Federigo and Alfonso moved swiftly north to attack at Poggio Imperiale.

An enormously impressive fortress commanding the entire valley, Poggio Imperiale had massive stone walls several feet thick; its cavernous storage places were sufficient to hold enough food to keep any army comfortable through a protracted siege. Astonishingly, it was taken by Alfonso and Federigo in a single day. ". . . observing the dust occasioned by the enemy's approach," Machiavelli wrote—and assuming the enemy's troops to be vast—the Florentine defenders turned and ran like rabbits, "leaving their ammunition, carriages, and artillery to be taken by the foe." This was cowardice incarnate, and the townspeople in Florence were stunned and frightened.

Then the enemy troops did a most remarkable thing. Instead of following up their advantage, chasing the demoralized Florentines and closing on the town of Florence itself, they stopped and secured Poggio Imperiale, turned around, marched south several miles, and laid siege to the tiny town of Colle. "Had [Alfonso] the duke of Calabria undauntedly pushed on," a modern historian has written, "he would almost certainly have held Florence at his mercy. But such boldness was not in the military style of the day."

Most modern historians have assumed that Alfonso could "have held Florence at his mercy" had he pressed on—and that may be true. But the question is not so easily decided. The terrain between Poggio Imperiale and San Casciano is rugged indeed, easy enough for retreating soldiers to run over if they have left their artillery behind, but extremely difficult for an advancing army to cross, with all its supplies and equipment. And if Alfonso were to get all the way to Florence, what would he have done then? However weak and demoralized the city may have been, it still was no simple matter to lay siege to it.

Alfonso may well have been delaying, with the thought that his allied army led by Girolamo Riario soon would be breaking through toward Florence from the north, so that two forces then could converge on the city. Alfonso was not quite the typical mercenary leader. He was, first, King Ferrante's son, and secondly, a very hungry young man. Had he thought that he could guarantee his fame and fortune by taking the supreme prize of Florence, he probably would have marched on the town. Whether or not he was right in his decision to hold back, we may never know; but it was a fateful decision for Florence.

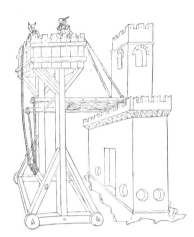

The sieges of fifteenth-century Italy generated substantial progress in warfare technology. With this mobile unit, for example, conceived by military strategist Robertus Valturius, a town could be bombarded and invaded simultaneously. Another design by Valturius (opposite) used a levered barrel.

The Duke settled his troops around the little town of Colle, and that, most assuredly, was a mistake. Colle is not situated among high mountains, but it is set upon the very peak of a small and unusually sheer mountain, so that any force attempting to take it must fight almost straight up into the sky. The Duke bombarded the town, and bombarded it, and bombarded it again—1,024 times according to the diarist Luca Landucci. Not until two months had passed did the little town finally drop from exhaustion and hunger, and by then it was too late. Riario's troops were moving from Imola toward Florence, through the mountains to the northeast, but Alfonso's army was too weary to turn back on Florence. Besides, winter had come; it was time for the seasonal truce. The warriors retired once again to their winter quarters.

The pressures of the war on Florence had become unbearable. The expense of the war was a burden; its damage to business, insupportable—and the plague was sending citizens scurrying out of the city to the country. Florence needed a brilliant diplomatic stroke to end the war, and Lorenzo worked to provide it.

In November, 1479, as the troops retired from the field, Lorenzo received hints that King Ferrante of Naples was willing to see him and discuss terms of peace. Through various secret diplomatic channels, Lorenzo satisfied himself that Ferrante was sincere, and in early December he boarded a boat at Pisa and sailed down the coast into the heart of the enemy camp.

Lorenzo needed to accomplish two objectives in his trip to Naples: first, to end the war; and second, to end it in such a way that the Florentines, and with luck, all Italians, would look on him as a hero. The second objective was no less important than the first, for if he gained a great reputation, it would be his best insurance that no one would try again to unseat him or to enter war against Florence lightheartedly. And thus, although he had made many thorough and cautious preparations with Ferrante, he kept them a secret from the Florentines. After his departure, a letter that he had written was read to the government in Florence:

Most Illustrious My Lords, . . . it seemed to me that the agitated and disturbed condition of our city demands acts and not words. I conceive that she desires, and indeed has extreme need of peace. Seeing that all other endeavors have been fruitless, I have determined to run some peril in my own person rather than expose the city to disaster. Therefore . . . I have decided to go openly to

COLLE DI VALDELSA

Alfonso, Duke of Calabria, and his troops march into the town of Colle in the climactic event of the papal-Neapolitan war against Florence. At the head of their standards is the papal banner, with its miter and key insignia.

Naples. Being the one most hated and persecuted by our enemies I may by placing myself in their hands be the means of restoring peace to our city. . . . If His Majesty the King intends to attack our liberty it seems to me well to know the worst quickly, and that one should be injured rather than the many. I am most glad to be that one. . . . having a greater position and larger stake in our city, not only than I deserve but probably than any citizen in our days, I am more bound than any other man to give up all to my country, even my life. . . . My ardent wish is that either my life or my death . . . should contribute to the good of our city. . . . Should evil befall me I shall not complain . . .

He certainly cast himself in the role of hero, and the Florentines were deliciously frightened for him and thrilled. No other single act won as much credit for Lorenzo throughout Italy, nothing else so confirmed his epithet, The Magnificent. Florence buzzed with talk of Piccinino, an ambassador from another state who had visited Ferrante on other business, and for his pains, had been coldly murdered by the King of Naples.

Recent historians, offended by Lorenzo's craftiness and guile over his trip to Naples, have tended to play down the danger to him and to play up his advance preparations, dismissing his trip as a sort of grand public relations junket. But even though Lorenzo was intentionally melodramatic about it, there was considerable risk. He had no more guarantee of safety than what amounted to a gentleman's agreement with the Mafia.

If Lorenzo knew anything, he knew how to behave like a diplomat. He had made friendships in Naples when his father had sent him touring Italy as a young man, and he had kept those friendships—with Ferrante's son Federigo, with Alfonso's cultivated wife, and especially with Diomede Carafa, King Ferrante's chief councilor. Lorenzo had been kind to Carafa on several occasions and once had given him an ancient bronze horse's head, one of the finest antiques discovered up to that time. No doubt, Carafa now interceded with the King for Lorenzo. But Lorenzo left nothing to chance. He curried the favor of the people, too, by such majestic gestures as freeing and giving clothing to galley slaves, staging banquets for the Neapolitan nobles, and giving marriage dowries to young girls.

His approach to Ferrante must have been as multifaceted as his approach to the Neapolitan people. It is certain that Lorenzo would have argued for peace from precedents of history and from the principles of Greek philosophy, holding up to Ferrante's consideration the great leaders of the past who sought peace rather than war. And he must have argued in terms of hard, realistic politics: Florence conquered was of no use to Naples, but Florence saved would be a good ally. Most popes were historically undependable—likely to turn against their own allies whenever it suited their purpose. But a combination of Florence, Milan, and Naples could be held together, not just by paper agreements, but by that most certain guarantor of alliances: self-interest.

Lorenzo actually was in no position to bargain. Ferrante had all the trump cards. And while they negotiated, the Florentine town of Sarzana fell—an upset, it was believed, engineered by Alfonso. Was Ferrante only talking for time? Was he, while keeping Lorenzo in Naples for three months, still trying to gain a military victory? He was unquestionably a treacherous man, and that possibility could not be overlooked. Lorenzo had presented his dozens of arguments, and Ferrante had agreed to a treaty, but he would not sign one.

Impatient—and again impulsive—Lorenzo decided to bluff. Saying he no longer could stay away from Florence, he abruptly bid Ferrante good-by and set out for home. Ferrante, still angling for time, sent a letter asking Lorenzo to return to Naples. Lorenzo ignored the letter: it was up to Ferrante to sign the treaty or not; Lorenzo was through with talking.

His delaying tactics exhausted, Ferrante signed the treaty.

Lorenzo was welcomed back to Florence with unalloyed joy. He had done what armies could not do. He had risked his life for his city and brought back an honorable peace. The sacred figure of the Madonna was carried through the city in procession. Trade revived, and inflation vanished. And sometime later Sandro Botticelli began work on his painting of Pallas and the Centaur, symbolizing wisdom conquering brutish chaos, in commemoration of Lorenzo's triumph.

Italy did not live happily ever after. Treaty or no treaty, Alfonso remained ominously in Siena, his armed presence there a cause for constant anxiety on Lorenzo's part. And Pope Sixtus refused to honor the treaty. Unable to fight, he still was unwilling to make peace.

Then a totally unexpected blow fell upon the Pope. The Turks invaded Italy. As Machiavelli reported it, part of the Emperor Mohammed II's army "under the Pasha Achmet, approached Velona, and, either from observing the facility of the enterprise, or in obedience to his sovereign's commands, coasting along the Italian shores, [Achmet] suddenly landed four thousand soldiers, and attacked the city of Otranto, which he easily took, plundered, and put all the inhabitants to the sword. He then fortified the city and port, and having assembled a large body of cavalry, pillaged the surrounding country."

The Turks threatened to gobble up the whole countryside, and the Pope was thoroughly alarmed. He called upon all Italians to unite and fight off the common enemy. He extended his hand to Florence and offered them forgiveness,

Pallas and the Centaur, *by Sandro Botticelli, celebrates the return of peace after Lorenzo's treaty with the King of Naples. The goddess of wisdom—entwined in the olive branches of peace—subdues the armed centaur.*

which the Florentines promptly accepted. And Alfonso gathered his troops and marched off to Otranto to battle the Turks. The attack at Otranto was such a fortuitous event for Lorenzo that some accused him of arranging it, but more likely it was simply a stroke of extraordinary luck.

Once the Turks were repulsed—easily, and almost singlehandedly, by Alfonso—Florence regained most of its lost territory and began to enjoy genuine security. Yet peace did not reign. With the hope still of aggrandizing Girolamo Riario, Sixtus combined with Venice to attack Ferrara. This time Lorenzo and Ferrante sent troops to maintain peace. Next, Sixtus declared war against Venice, and again Lorenzo brought the disputants to the conference table to conclude peace. This, the Peace of Bagnolo, concluded in 1484, was the last frustration Pope Sixtus was able to endure. The day after he received news of the peace, he

When the forces of Emperor Mohammed II invaded the town of Otranto in 1480, the warring factions of Italy suddenly were united in an effort to drive the Turks from the peninsula. The contemporary drawing at right shows four nobles leading their separate armies in the common cause that united even Lorenzo and Pope Sixtus. As soon as the Turks were beaten, however, the unity promptly disintegrated.

died—unable, it was said, to face happily the prospect of life without war.

Lorenzo now dedicated himself to trying to keep Italy from exploding. He had returned to his grandfather's triple alliance among Naples, Milan, and Florence, one created by the Peace of Lodi in 1454. The Peace of Lodi had included a curious paragraph, one specifying that the signers would work together to maintain peace and that they would take united action, as the modern historian Ferdinand Schevill has written, "against any member state guilty of disturbing it."

Lorenzo took the hint from the Peace of Lodi, and from it he developed a conscious policy of maintaining all the states of Italy in a balance of power. That he had hit upon a forceful notion is undeniable, for the concept of balance of power politics has ruled international diplomacy to our own day.

Still Italy was not at peace. While Lorenzo could help to keep it from total chaos, he could not bring it an enduring peace. Indeed, he was forced himself to enter minor wars, and he occasionally found himself obstructing peaceful settlements. There were times when he could do nothing else, for the Italians of his day were determined to have strife. The internal battling for control of Florence, the assassinations, the "international" jostling for power, the fighting, the sight of mercenaries traipsing over the Italian countryside—none of these are unique to the story of Lorenzo. They are, rather, the background; they form a representative picture of all Italy during the Renaissance.

The old world of feudalism was breaking up; a new world of business and politics and philosophy was being born. There were, it seemed, no rules by which men could live, save the few guidelines that they had revived from ancient Greece and Rome. Figuratively—and as it turned out later, literally—they were on a voyage of discovery, without charts or compasses, not knowing their destination, with an unruly crew understandably anxious, ready to break into mutiny at any moment—if not for a cause, then simply from anxiety or to test the limits that bound them.

Lorenzo emerged from this background, and particularly from the Pazzi war, not only the undisputed leader of Florence, but quite clearly, the foremost leader in Italy as well. He was by that time the established peacemaker of all Italy; thereafter, when Italian states came into conflict, they turned to Lorenzo to serve as arbiter. He was, for better or worse, captain of that storm-tossed ship of states.

Reflected in this detail from a Giovanni Bellini painting, the murder of innocent wayfarers by brutal mercenary soldiers was a problem of almost epidemic proportions in fifteenth-century Italy.

IV   THE VIRTUOUS PRINCE

"A certain hermit came to the house of Lorenzo de' Medici at the Poggio a Caiano," Luca Landucci wrote in his diary several years after the Pazzi conspiracy, "and the servants declared that he intended to murder Lorenzo, so they took him and sent him to the Bargello [the prison], and he was put to the rack."

Eighteen days later, Landucci reports, "This hermit died at Santa Maria Novella, having been tortured in various ways. It was said that they skinned the soles of his feet, and then burnt them by holding them in the fire till the fat dripped off them; after which they set him upright and made him walk across the great hall; and these things caused his death. Opinions were divided as to whether he were guilty or innocent."

Another time, a young man who had killed a public official was being taken to prison. A crowd gathered and shouted to him to run while they tried to beat off the guards. Lorenzo entered the piazza where the uproar occurred, had the young man sent off to be hanged, and had four of the crowd whipped and exiled.

Lorenzo rarely walked the streets of Florence alone: he was accompanied by ten armed men, one of whom marched out in front bearing a naked sword. His spies kept him informed of the machinations of potential enemies, and when several conspirators hatched a plot in Rome to assassinate him, they were found out and promptly were hanged. They had not, it was noted, attempted assassination, but mere scheming against Lorenzo's life had come to be considered high treason.

He made certain that no marriages were contracted of which he did not approve, thus assuring that his own alli-

In the prime of life, at the apex of his power, Lorenzo de' Medici sat for this painted terra-cotta bust by Andrea del Verrocchio. Every feature emphasizes Lorenzo's characteristic boldness, ruthlessness, and imagination.

ances were strengthened through family ties—and that enemy alliances were frustrated. Some of Lorenzo's controls on Florentine life were so severe—he interfered at times in even the most unimportant marriages—that one can only suspect that he still harbored a profound bitterness over the murder of his brother, Giuliano.

Without doubt, something had changed dramatically in Florence since the Pazzi conspiracy and war.

Florence emerged from the war with its finances in near-shambles, and the pressures of diplomacy constantly demanded more and more money. Between 1482 and 1487 the treasury was drained of 818,000 florins for additional military expeditions. Florentine finances had long been in a delicate condition. Coupled now with a general decline in economic activity in Italy, and the enormous expenses incurred during the Pazzi war and immediately after, Florence faced a very real crisis. Several extreme measures were necessary, and Lorenzo decided first to draw money from the city's dowry fund and secondly to place the administration of the "treasury" of the republic more firmly in the hands of the wealthy families of Florence.

In the past, other leaders often had dipped into the dowry fund. In Lorenzo's own time the Volterra war had caused the government to take money from the fund, and a huge sum was taken out again at the beginning of the Pazzi war. It was a tender point with Florentines, for it affected the very foundation of the family.

The dowry fund worked quite simply: when a girl was born, her father would put money into the state's dowry fund. By making continued payments, and collecting interest on the money as well, he was able to provide his daughter with a dowry when she was ready to marry. We have remarked upon the importance of the family and of marriage in Italy. It remains only to be noted that good marriages could not be arranged without good dowries. For the state to default on these payments, or to reduce them drastically, meant that aspiring families could not improve their social and economic position through marriage. Nothing cut Florentines to the quick more than this tampering with the dowry fund. And during Lorenzo's lifetime this was to become the most frequently and most vociferously criticized of his actions.

The second measure, placing control of finances in the hands of already wealthy men, was inescapable. Only the wealthy could provide big loans on short notice to meet such crises as the Pazzi war. But the effect of the govern-

Well-bred brides, wealthy bride-grooms, and substantial dowries went hand in hand in fifteenth-century Florence, exemplified by this very elaborate wedding chest.

ment's reliance on the wealthy—and of the steep interest payments made for their loans—was to concentrate more and more power in their hands. Perhaps worse than that, it meant that the rich got richer and the poor got poorer. There was a graduated income tax in Florence. Lorenzo paid as much as sixty-six per cent of his income in taxes. But even so, capital tended to be drained from the lower classes and paid in debt interest to the upper classes.

In fact, the financial measures instituted after the Pazzi war finally got Florence onto a relatively sound economic footing. Between 1488 and 1494, taxes decreased, the dowry fund was fairly well stabilized, and peace kept the aristocrats from skimming off too much in the way of interest on loans. However, because Lorenzo knew that the measures would be unpopular, he first made certain that he held the reins of government even more securely before he rearranged the finances of the city.

Lorenzo's constitutional reform, effected almost the moment that he returned from Naples, was meant not to abolish any of the existing councils of government, but to add

Lorenzo's Florence was an international marketplace. In the illustration above, a housewife buys her day's supply of indispensable olive oil from a passing peddler.

yet another council with two powerful committees. This was called the Council of the Seventy, and it held all powers of government; its members were rich Medici partisans who sat for life. They appointed two committees: the Eight, who administered foreign and military affairs, and the Twelve, who dealt with commerce and finance. Lorenzo himself was a member of the Seventy—thus breaking the Medici tradition of staying in the background—and he became a political boss who ruled with a steel fist in an iron glove.

Lorenzo was driven to this new, more rigid role in Florence because realities had dictated it. He had to keep Florence from bankruptcy, and he had to be tough in order to do it. His power never was complete, however, and it often was challenged. There is no evidence to prove that Lorenzo ever bribed his fellow Florentines; still, he probably did. The lack of evidence rather indicates that he was very accomplished at keeping his bribes a secret. He certainly dispensed patronage. Nonetheless, the linchpin of his position in Florence was the influence that he had with other European leaders. Above all, the kind of freedom that Florentines knew and desired was freedom from foreign domination, and they felt that Lorenzo, on whom the other Italian leaders looked as a prince, was their surest defender of that liberty. Lorenzo himself often emphasized to foreign rulers that there were limitations on his powers, that he was only a citizen of Florence, and that he always had to "conform to the will of the majority." Yet the will of the majority was to give Lorenzo tremendous room in which to move and deal. In the final analysis, he ruled as much and as far as the Florentines wanted him to—and that was quite a lot.

However tough and ruthless Lorenzo became to ensure his security, his actions still were tempered with civility. He recalled from exile the families who had attempted to overthrow his grandfather. The Albizzi, by then, had suffered the worst that fortune had to offer and never again played a significant role in Florence. But the Strozzi family, who had been involved with the Albizzi, had nursed their money carefully, and Filippo Strozzi had started a bank in Naples and had acquired a substantial fortune. Returning to Florence, Filippo prudently avoided feuding with Lorenzo and thus came to play a large part in the history of Florence.

It was Filippo who started to build the spacious Strozzi palace in Florence. Before construction work started, he wisely sent the plans for the building to Lorenzo for his advice. The original design called for a row of shops on the bottom floor—for extra income, Filippo said. In truth, it

The busy cheese kitchen above was one of many dispensaries of farm produce to be found in the country-side near Florence. Staple goods, such as rice (left), were sold in stalls that lined the city streets.

would seem that the shops were intended to keep the Strozzi palace modest in appearance, to keep it less imposing than the Medici palace. It was cunning of Filippo to send the plans to Lorenzo. Lorenzo returned them with the advice to forget the shops and give the palace the bold façade that has won the building so much praise through the centuries.

Lorenzo's system of personally administered justice is hardly the ideal of freedom to which we are accustomed today. Yet, in his time, Florence was the most democratically free state in Italy. The Florentines had read the Roman poet Claudian: *Numquam libertas gratior extat, quam sub rege pio;* "liberty is never sweeter than when it is protected by a virtuous prince."

It was a good time to be alive. It lasted only a short time, but those dozen years—1480 to 1492—were the golden age of Lorenzo's Florence. There were plays and music

A Roman colonnade, a scene from a tale in Boccaccio's Decameron, *and perhaps above all else, a splendid banquet—these elements, incorporated in Sandro Botticelli's painting, characterize the interests and tastes of the Florentine aristocracy during its golden age under the rule of the Medici.*

The Florentines were not incapable of donning rose-colored glasses. In the engraving at left, the rather gruesome myth of Bacchus and Ariadne is retold as though it all had taken place aboard a mobile bed of vines and grapes.

and horse races and grand celebrations on the feast days. The traditional festival began on May Day, with dancing and singing in the streets, and the fireworks and masked balls and feasts and tourneys went on almost constantly for the next two months, until the feast of San Giovanni, St. John, the patron saint of Florence.

For San Giovanni's Day, the shops were decorated with silk and gold cloth, and for several days before it there would be processions and parades through the streets. Then on the day itself there would be a hundred gilded towers carved with figures of horsemen and soldiers and dancing girls—representing the tribute of Florence's subject cities. The palace of the Signoria was awash in banners; great giants walked about on stilts, and plays and pantomimes were performed in which angels battled devils and ancient pagan creatures appeared with nymphs and astrologers and boisterous choruses of singers: Bacchus, the Greek god of wine; Paris and Ariadne; and Eros, dressed in swaddling clothes. Lorenzo wrote songs. The architect Brunelleschi designed sets and produced astonishing theatrical effects, such as a celestial sphere filled with flashing lights and flying angels from which the angel Gabriel himself descended to earth. One of the greatest designers for these revels was the painter Piero di Cosimo, who was to design a grisly Triumph of Death for one such occasion. Death stood in a wagon with bones and white crosses painted on its sides and surrounded by coffins and torches. When the wagon stopped, strange figures costumed to look like skeletons got out and

sang unearthly chants to the accompaniment of the trumpets of doom. It was terrifying—and wonderful.

As you make your way along the streets [one Florentine reported of one of the festivals], the houses are all hung with tapestries, and the chairs and benches covered with taffeta. Everywhere you see girls and young women dressed in silk and bedizened with jewels, precious stones and pearls. . . . The whole city, that day, is given over to revelry and feasting, with so many fifes and music, songs, dances, and other festivities and merry-making, that this earth seems like a paradise.

Then there was the day that the Sultan of Egypt sent a menagerie of animals, including a lion and a giraffe. There

was a great parade, and the Florentines gawked unembarrassedly: they never had seen a giraffe before. "Her picture can be seen painted in many parts of Florence," Landucci wrote, "as she lived here for many years."

Despite such high spirits, prosperity was threatened. Lorenzo called in the state galleys that had monopolized the trade to the Levant and so encouraged private ships to take a greater share of trading profits. Cheap woolen goods from Lombardy were permitted into the Pisan territory, thus keeping the working classes better clothed and warmer. Trade with England thrived, and new trade agreements were worked out with the East. Construction finally began

ALTA PALMI CCCIIII

NEW YORK PUBLIC LIBRARY

One of the proudest possessions of the Florentines was a giraffe —a gift to Lorenzo from the Sultan of Egypt. The people of the city never had seen one before.

on the Strozzi palace, continuing a building boom that had begun in 1450. Between 1450 and the Pazzi conspiracy thirty new palaces were built in Florence, all of the characteristic rugged stone. Florence was, indeed, a city of stone; even the poorest homeowner built in stone. In the narrow, twisting stone streets, and in the fifty broad sunny piazzas, business hummed.

The center of business was Or San Michele, once the site of a granary, now a small gem of a church. Around it the offices of the bankers were grouped. In good weather, like all Florentines, the bankers stayed outside, setting up tables in the street to change money and negotiate loans. Nearby, the cloth and silk merchants had their offices. And around the corner was the market, buzzing with trade over vegetables and meats and fruits. Radiating from that center were the shops and offices of the goldsmiths, the furniture makers, and candlemakers. The street names remain to remind Florentines today of the old shape of the city: Via dei Saponai, the street of the soapmakers; Via dei Speziali, the street of the druggists; Via dell' Ariento, named for the silversmiths. There were twenty-one guilds in Florence. The seven greater guilds represented the judges, the cloth importers and manufacturers, the retailers and merchants, the bankers, the furriers, the druggists, and the doctors. The fourteen minor guilds represented the butchers, bakers, and tanners, the builders and woodworkers, the winedealers and innkeepers, and the smaller shopkeepers and businessmen. Each of the guilds had a *gonfalonier*, a banner bearer, who proudly carried the banner of his guild in the countless parades and festivals in Florence.

A merchant named Benedetto Dei several years earlier had expressed the confidence, not to say overconfidence, that his fellow Florentines enjoyed. To a Venetian friend Dei wrote:

Florence is more beautiful and five hundred forty years older than your Venice. We spring from triply noble blood. We are one-third Roman, one-third Frankish, and one-third Fiesolan. . . . We have round about us thirty thousand estates . . . yielding us yearly bread and meat, wine and oil, vegetables and cheese, hay and wood, to the value of nine hundred thousand ducats in cash, as you Venetians, Genoese, Chians, and Rhodians who come to buy them know well enough. We have two trades [wool and silk] greater than any four of yours in Venice put together.

Florence trades with the entire world, Dei said—with no trace of modesty, false or real. He listed wool shops (two hundred seventy of them), warehouses of the silk merchants (eighty-three "rich and splendid" ones), cabinetmakers, "whose business is carving and inlaid work" (eighty-four),

As the illustration below from a fifteenth-century Florentine manuscript shows, shipping was a subject of great interest to Florence. With no port of its own, the city always was pressed to maintain its pathways to the sea and to port cities on the Italian coast that prospered from Florentine commerce.

artists, apothecaries, grocers and butchers, and goldsmiths. "It would awaken the dead in its praise," Dei triumphantly concluded.

Florence had everything, and not the least of its strengths was its citizens, with their blissful belief that they and their city surpassed almost anything that ever had touched earth. It came perilously close to unbridled arrogance, yet it rarely turned sour. If Lorenzo helped to make Florence, he also reflected its temper exactly. Like Lorenzo, most Florentines felt that the opportunities open to them were unlimited. Movable-type printing was invented in Germany in the mid-fifteenth century. Some books printed by German printers fell into the hands of a Florentine goldsmith, Bernardo Cennini. He looked them over, thought about them, and then sat down, made his own type, and published Servius' *Commentary on Vergil's Bucolics*. "To the mind of a Florentine," he wrote as an introduction to this first book, "nothing is difficult."

Prosperity could not last, and it did not. While the fifteenth century was a period of ups and downs in the economic history of Europe, it was, generally speaking, a century of economic depression, a depression that deepened after 1470 and lasted well into the next century. Turmoil in the East and a general shrinking of international trade were the immediate causes, and the depression struck even at the wealthy banker-art patrons of Florence. In 1399 there were seventy-one banks in Florence; in 1460 there were thirty-three. By 1490, there were not enough bankers

Like the guilds of medieval Europe, Florence's professional groups often contributed works of art to public buildings and churches. Their donations were recorded by insignia placed near their gifts. At the church of Or San Michele the gifts of (left to right) the masons and carpenters, physicians and apothecaries, and silk manufacturers were noted on these plaques made by Lucca and Andrea della Robbia.

to fill the offices of the banking guild (Arte del Cambio), and by 1520, only seven banks were left.

The Medici bank had reached its apogee between 1435 and 1455, under the management of Cosimo. After Cosimo's death it began a decline, owing in part to a lack of the strong, careful control that Cosimo had exerted and in larger part to the broad economic conditions of Europe. After the Pazzi conspiracy in 1478, the Medici bank went into steady and rapid decline, and although Lorenzo has been blamed for neglecting the business, it seems unlikely that even Cosimo's financial wizardry could have saved it by then.

The Medici bank performed a wide range of services: taking deposits, transferring funds from city to city and country to country, making loans, and collecting revenues. A good part of the fortune was based upon taking a fee for collecting the revenues of the Church. There were branches throughout Italy, in Rome, Venice, Milan, Naples, and Pisa; and there were branches as well in London, Bruges, Geneva, Lyon, Basel, and Avignon. Because the branches were deployed so widely, and because communications were painfully slow, branch managers necessarily were given vast powers to make decisions on their own. They bought and sold wool and spices and oil; they acted as agents for clients who wanted to buy silver and jewels; and they dabbled in local politics.

Just as the ancient banking families often had been ruined by making loans to losing political leaders, so was

The gold florin, currency of the Medici bank, became the international symbol of fiscal stability —much as the dollar is today.

the Medici bank dealt several devastating blows by branch managers who had not learned that lesson of history. Tommaso Portinari, a member of an old, distinguished Florentine family, was the worst culprit.

The manager of the Medici bank's Bruges branch, Portinari was a highly talented banker with one fatal fault: he loved to gamble. He gambled on Duke Charles of Burgundy, known as Charles the Rash, and advanced huge sums of money to help Charles in his campaign to create an independent state between France and Germany. Unfortunately, the reckless Charles got himself killed in battle in 1477, and Portinari's investment could not be collected.

The manager in London—inspired, and perhaps even encouraged by Portinari—hazarded huge loans to King Edward IV. Unhappily, this was a time of civil war, the Wars of the Roses. Edward IV was too much preoccupied to get around to repaying the loan.

Lorenzo was forced at first to send large amounts of florins to London and Bruges to bail out his branches, and finally, at the time of the Pazzi conspiracy, he had to liquidate the two branches.

In the meantime, at Lyon, the simple incompetence of Lionetto de' Rossi was sending that branch toward bankruptcy. In spite of the fact that King Louis XI enriched the Lyon branch by favoring it with his business, Rossi bungled the management, and Lorenzo had to reorganize the branch. There was a brief period of prosperity until Louis died in 1483, and then, inexplicably, the depositors panicked and started a run on the bank—which forced Lorenzo once again to reorganize the branch at a considerable loss.

The Rome branch was the one of greatest importance to the Medici bank, providing much of the profit and most of the working capital for the entire Medici business empire. It was run by Lorenzo's uncle Giovanni Tornabuoni, who alternately wrote to his nephew in fawning abjectness ("I have God in heaven and Your Magnificence on earth") and engaged in tempestuous quarrels. An unsteady man, he kept himself in check only by following conventions and thus ran the Rome branch both haphazardly and dully, finally letting it slip pitifully toward bankruptcy.

The worst blow dealt to the Rome branch was, of course,

Opposite is a page from Nicola Valori's manuscript The Life of Lorenzo. *At top left the author presents the biography to Pope Leo X, Lorenzo's son; the Pontiff's combined papal and Medici coat of arms is at the bottom. In the rondel at right is an unusual portrait of Lorenzo—smiling.*

IN NOBI
LISSIMA
MEDICVM
FAMILIA
MVLTIPRE
CLARIMA
GNIQ3 VI
RIFVERE
INQVIBVS
IOANNES MEDICES QVI
MAGNO ET INVICTO ợ
ANIMO VICECOMITIBVS

Sese opponeus sæpius patriæ Nostræ
libertatem & communem omnium sa
lutem tutatus est. Verius quoq in
Equestri dignitate quæ prima apud
florentinos habetur sine controuersia
princeps Nostræ quoad uixit Rei p̃
extitit rector et gubernator Quid sos
mus Ille Magnus qui in magnis cłı

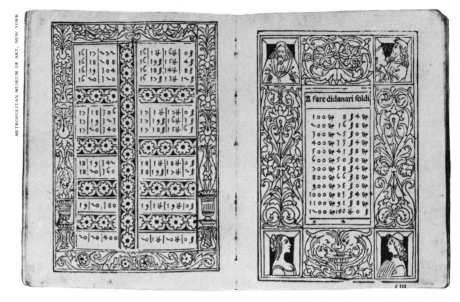

the Pazzi conspiracy, when the Pope denied his debt to the bank and seized the alum stocks in the possession of the Medici. In the wake of that misfortune the Medici banks closed in Milan (1478), Avignon (1479), and Venice (1481). Curiously enough, Renato de' Pazzi, the best businessman in that family, knew that the Rome branch under Tornabuoni's management was in trouble even before the conspiracy—and for that reason refused to take part in the plot. The Medici bank was headed for bankruptcy, he felt, and if the Pazzi simply waited long enough, the Medici would lose their fortune and therefore lose their power in Florence.

The bank's biggest problem was at the very top, with its general manager, Francesco Sassetti. Sassetti, charged with overseeing all the branch managers, was a man who hated unpleasantness and avoided it at the cost of not settling arguments between his managers and not imposing his will on them with any forcefulness. When the adventurer Tommaso Portinari embarked on his wild schemes in Bruges, and cautious advisers urged Sassetti to bring him back into line, Sassetti simply refused to listen. Nor would he hear any criticism of Lionetto de' Rossi in Lyon, until it was too late. At the end of his career, Sassetti wrote Lorenzo a letter: "I should not omit to tell you that, if your managerial staff is not ruled with more discipline and greater firmness than in times past, trouble will recur because any relaxation of authority is a tempting bait which leads to license and unruliness." Indeed, it is in character that the weak-willed

Under the influence of the Medici the arts played a role even in the business life of Florence. The arithmetic tables and currency-conversion charts of today's merchant would be printed in a functional, plain booklet; but in Florence they were incorporated in the richly embellished manuscript shown above. The Medici bank, as drawn below by the artist Filarete, was a rugged, impressive Neoclassical structure with the Medici coat of arms repeated between arched windows.

Sassetti tried to keep his nose clean by pointing out his own mistakes as though someone else had made them.

Ultimately, of course, the blame for the failure of the Medici bank must be laid to Lorenzo. Once, when pressed to countermand an order of Sassetti's, he admitted that "he did not understand such matters," and it is clear that business was not Lorenzo's strong suit. He can be blamed for not staffing his bank with men of more forceful character. That he did not is difficult to explain: perhaps there simply were no men in Florence dynamic enough to take hold of the Medici bank and navigate against the adverse stream of general depression.

There can be no doubt that, at the depth of the Pazzi conspiracy, with his banks toppling and ever-increasing demands being made on his resources, Lorenzo dipped his hand into the funds of the government to shore up his own fortunes. It was a maneuver that Renato de' Pazzi had not counted on when he predicted Lorenzo's bankruptcy before the conspiracy.

Lorenzo's enemies were outraged at his theft, and later reports of his personal use of public funds became exaggerated. It is probable that Lorenzo stole from the state no more than he spent of his own fortune from time to time—for entertaining foreign leaders, bribing diplomats, and traveling on state business. Since he used money as one of his biggest weapons in diplomacy, his own funds and those of his banks necessarily became entangled with public funds. Then, too, there was the very real danger that if the worldwide Medici banking empire fell, important as it was

This fifteenth-century woodcut print shows some of the business activities of a Florentine bank.

Representatives of the Medici bank were encouraged to patronize the arts when they went abroad. The agent Portinari commissioned the Flemish master Hugo van der Goes to paint a triptych; the central panel is pictured above. The representative's own likeness was included on one of the side panels; he is the kneeling figure in the detail on the page opposite.

to Florence's economy, Florence itself might have plunged into a deep depression.

The fact remains, however, that Lorenzo stole—and while he was at it, he stole a lot. His enemies were not disposed to look kindly on the matter: he was repeatedly attacked as a callous political boss who stole public funds, a tyrant who ruled only in his own selfish interest. Such was the vitriol with which the charge was made that it has stuck to Lorenzo to our own day, and even the most sympathetic historians betray an uneasiness and embarrassment when they discuss this aspect of Lorenzo's political career.

What Lorenzo had discovered is what the banking families of a century or two before had discovered—the inherent vicious circle in Renaissance business. Wealth brings political power; political power brings obligations to support foreign leaders, to support them even against the best interests of personal business; and support of political leaders is a risky proposition that brings bankruptcy. The circle is complete.

What Lorenzo needed to do was remove himself from the failing banking and trade markets of Europe. He needed to find a more secure basis for his fortune—and that is precisely what he attempted to do toward the end of his life. With his great love of the country, it was natural for him to turn to farming and real estate for security for his money. Slowly, in these last dozen years, he drew his money out of banking and bought farmland around Florence. Had he been quicker, he might have succeeded in saving the family fortune. But fate was one step ahead of him.

It often happens that men who thrive under truly great challenges are merely impatient with vexing details. Lorenzo's sense of the dramatic was superb, and he felt at home only on a very large stage. Yet, after the Pazzi war was ended, he found himself constrained more and more to acting on the irritatingly small stage of Florentine politics and business. He came to fret over trifles, as this letter concerning a trivial personal matter shows: "For the love of God, Baccio, bestir yourself with all your might in this matter. I am most anxious about it. . . . I long for peace at home as I see small reason to hope for it abroad."

The gout had begun to bother him, and he had to leave Florence for extended stays at the soothing baths. His mistress, Lucrezia, died in 1488, and so too did his wife, Clarice —leaving him deeply saddened. Politics and business had never been his greatest loves, and now they became nothing but annoyances. "A friend told me," an ambassador to Florence wrote home to his chief, "that at home His Magnificence talks like a desperate man, and says that he would like to go for six months to some place where Italian affairs would never be mentioned. . . . One can only conceive that His Magnificence is very irate. . . ."

He longed to be in the country. He longed to be riding and hunting. He longed to do nothing but spend hour after hour, day after day, listening to music, writing poetry, and talking to his friends Poliziano, Pico, Landino, and Marsilio Ficino—his friends of the Platonic Academy, the humanists.

V

VITA PLOTI
NI ET EIVS.
LIBRI·LIIII·A
MARSILIO
FICINO TRA
DVCTI ET EX
POSITI AD
MAGNANI
MVM·LAV
RENTIVM
MEDICEM
PATRIAE
SERVATOREM

PROHEMIVM MARS
TINI IN LIBROS PLC
NIMVM LAVRENT
PATRIAE SERV

96

THE HUMANISTS

Man is the measure of all things: not God, not nature, not any abstract force, but man. Man shall be free; he shall be who he wishes, what he wills. Are there impersonal laws or forces of history? Man makes history and the laws of history; let history be changed, let the laws be rewritten to suit man. Are there natural barriers to man's wishes—are there broad oceans, do the stars influence his destiny? Let the oceans be crossed, the stars denied. The world must be made to fit man, not man to fit the world. Does the Church impose limits on man's full realization of himself? Let it be shown that the Church does not understand the intentions of God.

"I have set you at the center of the world," Lorenzo's friend Pico della Mirandola has God saying to man, "so that from there you may more easily survey whatever is in the world. We have made you neither heavenly nor earthly, neither mortal nor immortal, so that more freely and more honorably the moulder and maker of yourself, you may fashion yourself in whatever form you shall prefer."

Such is the basis of humanism, a view of man that informs all of the Western world today, a view of man that underlies our political freedoms, our liberal philosophies, and even, in an age on which organized religion seems to have lost its hold, a view of man that justifies many of our moral beliefs. Humanism developed in the Middle Ages, nurtured by men like Dante and Petrarch, and reached its full flower during the Renaissance, encouraged by such men as Lorenzo de' Medici.

Humanism is founded upon—indeed it requires—a tremendous confidence in man and his potential. It is a way of thinking that exalts, and exults in, the universal man, the

Florence received much of the dogma of humanism from Marsilio Ficino's treatise on the life and work of Plotinus, a third-century Roman philosopher. Dedicated to Lorenzo, Ficino's manuscript bears the Medici shield.

Although scholarship and humanistic studies received great impetus in Lo-renzo's Florence, the revival of learning had its roots in the late Middle Ages. This carving of Italian scholars dates from the fourteenth century.

man who develops all his talents, the generalist, the non-conformist, the individualist. The man to be admired is *l'uomo singolare*, the singular man; and the man to be admired above all is *l'uomo unico*, the unique man.

It is, however, a kind of thinking that can go wrong: Fondolo of Cremona once had a chance to push the Pope and the Emperor of the Holy Roman Empire off a high tower and lived his entire life regretting that he had not done it—not because he disliked them, but because he had missed his golden opportunity to win fame by doing it. Similarly, one of the rulers of Siena made a pastime of recklessly flinging huge boulders from the top of a mountain.

Yet trust in the individual gives us one of our most prized ideals as well, for belief in individualism implies tolerance for all individuals—the very basis of humaneness. That trust, if we can believe Marsilio Ficino, created a golden age in Florence: If "we are to call any age golden, it is beyond doubt that. . . . such is true of this our age. . . . For this century, like a golden age, has restored to light the liberal arts, which were almost extinct: grammar, poetry, rhetoric, painting, sculpture, architecture, music, the ancient singing of songs to the Orphic lyre, and all this in Florence."

The first essential ingredient of this golden age of humanism was a revival, a rebirth, a "Renaissance" of the learning and ideals of antiquity. It depended first, therefore, upon the scholars who scoured the world for ancient manuscripts and rediscovered classical works on philosophy, architecture, politics, and the arts. It depended, secondly, upon multiplying those manuscripts, copying them by hand, and seeing that they were distributed around Italy to men who would read them, argue about them, and adapt the old ideas to new situations.

In the process of copying the old manuscripts, Poggio Bracciolini discarded the awkward Gothic script and imitated an older example of handwriting to create the very script that is the basis of modern handwriting. (Poggio invented, too, the justified line—the technique of making all lines on a page align vertically both left and right—a technique evident in the design of the pages of this book.) The introduction of printing at the beginning of Lorenzo's rule greatly accelerated the dissemination of knowledge, but even before Lorenzo's time, Cosimo de' Medici had commissioned hundreds of agents to find and copy books—and at the monastery of San Marco, beginning with eight hundred volumes, Cosimo, in 1444, opened the first public library in Europe.

Lorenzo recognized quite early in his career, at the age of twenty-three, that more than libraries would be required to keep humanism and the "humanities" flourishing, and in 1472 he persuaded the Florentine government to re-establish the moribund University of Pisa. The old university had languished for two centuries, and the Florentines were pleased that their own University of Florence had so far outstripped that of their subject town of Pisa. But Lorenzo was determined to make all of Florence's subject towns prosperous; he had promoted Pisa's commercial revival, and now he wished the town to be a center of learning as well. He split up the Florentine faculty, sent some of his leading professors to Pisa, directly supervised the hiring of more professors for the new university, and sent one of his own sons to study there. Later, the university's distinguished graduates would count Galileo among their number.

Cosimo had built a vast number of new buildings in Florence—churches, villas, and libraries. Lorenzo built only three: a monastery in San Gallo, a villa near Arezzo, and another villa at Poggio a Caiano. Poggio a Caiano was designed unlike any other villa. It had, first, a noble façade, with columns and frieze, like a Greek temple—a model that no one had thought of following before. It had, secondly, a vast domed room at the center, ideal for a large central library. Lorenzo never lived at the completed villa; it was not finished in his lifetime. And it appears that he never intended to live there as he did at his other villas. It was intended, rather, to be a study center for the leading scholars of the world, an Institute for Advanced Study—the first of its kind in the Western world.

The very heart of the humanist revival, however, was not a university, nor an institution of any kind. Indeed, it had no building of its own, no regular place of meeting. It

This painting of Lorenzo's villa at Poggio a Caiano reflects the Renaissance ideal of orderliness carried to extremes. The estate was more rustic than shown here.

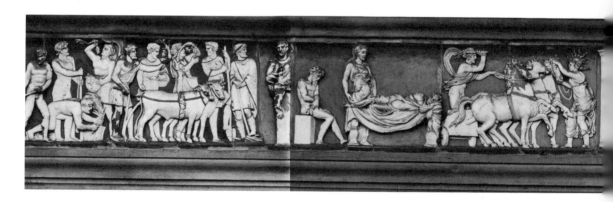

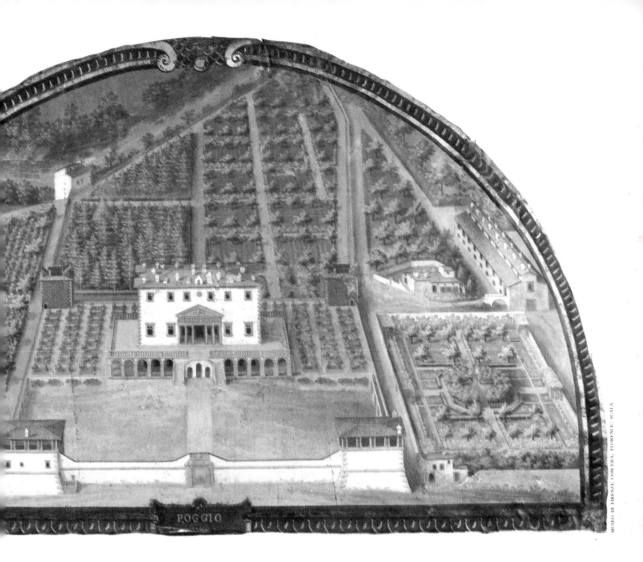

Clearly an imitation of Classical Greek friezes, the relief below, from the façade of Poggio a Caiano, depicts an agricultural gathering and a sad departure scene.

was an informal group of men who clustered around Lorenzo, dined with him, relaxed at his country villas, and corresponded with leaders and scholars throughout the world. It was called the Platonic Academy, and it existed only in the thoughts and conversations and writings of Marsilio Ficino, Pico della Mirandola, Angelo Poliziano, Lorenzo, and several other of Lorenzo's friends.

In 1439 Cosimo had met and talked to a bearded, eighty-three-year-old Greek named Gemistus Pletho, at that time the world's leading authority on the ancient Greek philosopher Plato. Cosimo was greatly taken with Gemistus, for in place of Aristotle—the authoritarian philosopher given to laying down absolute rules and the darling of the Fathers of the Church—Gemistus spoke of Plato. In Plato, Cosimo found a humane, sometimes troubled philosopher who sought truth through dialogue, through argument, sensible always of the contradictions of reality, the

101

Angelo Poliziano

Marsilio Ficino

turmoil of emotions. Plato was a philosopher who spoke directly to Cosimo and to the Renaissance: here was a thinker who understood that it was not enough to lay down an abstract Good, a man who knew that men must struggle through the conflicts of a tumultuous and often unjust world to achieve the ideals that they set for themselves.

It was not until 1459 that Cosimo was able to devote all the time he wished to the study of Plato's teachings. In that year he adopted the young Florentine Greek scholar Marsilio Ficino. He was a tiny, stammering young man, perhaps no more than five feet tall, slim and melancholy and deeply religious. Cosimo gave Marsilio a house and an income and commissioned the young man to translate all of Plato's works into Latin. The work took eighteen years to complete, and Ficino, according to the modern historian Vincent Cronin, was "the first man for many centuries to discover the historical Plato. It was an exciting discovery, a philosophic America." Ficino's lifelong labor was to create a grand, monumental anachronism: to relate Plato and the teachings of Christ, to combine the best of the ancient world with the best of his own, to find a sweet harmony in a man-centered universe. His way of thought is called Neo-Platonism.

Any student of philosophy will recognize immediately that the Neo-Platonism of the Renaissance was a philosophical hash. Compounded of the superstitions and mysticism that had crept into Platonism from the East, of the Platonic Academy's own wildly soaring imaginations, of the occult cabalistic philosophy of the Jews, tidbits of medieval thought, and dollops of dozens of other flotsams and jetsams and gewgaws of science and myth and theology, a systematic rational attack could easily reduce it to rubble.

The central tenet of Neo-Platonism was that the various gods spoken of in all times and places were in truth one and the same God and that the force that had brought Him to create the world was the force of love. It was maintained, further, that man can find his way to this source of love and create as God has created. Indeed, Ficino insisted, man can "become a god."

There was a corollary to this thesis, and a very important one: "all things that exist," Ficino wrote, "insofar as they exist, are true; and insofar as they possess some force, order, and purpose they are good."

Man in all his attributes is good and may become a god. Despite all the hodgepodge of theories that the Neo-Platonists used in arriving at this notion, the idea itself suddenly became a key to unlock the full powers of man. Being good, being godlike, man may exercise all his powers and be embarrassed by nothing in his nature. Thus the first, great nude figures since antiquity were painted and sculpted. Botticelli, in his *Birth of Venus* and *La Primavera*, celebrated Venus, goddess of love. And Lorenzo wrote poetry not in the old mold of Latin but in his own language, Italian, the "vulgar" tongue.

In the eyes of these "love people" of Florence (to heap yet one more anachronism upon Ficino's system of thought), anything was possible. Anxious to create a new world, attracted still by the early, mystical teachings of the Church, the Neo-Platonists had reconciled the past and the present —and created a doctrine of surpassing optimism for the future.

The most brilliant young man in the Platonic Academy was Giovanni Pico della Mirandola, born in 1463. A strikingly handsome young man, with golden hair and boundless energy, Pico had attended four universities by the age of eighteen, and he boasted that he knew twenty-two languages (although, in fact, he knew only the alphabets of some of them). He studied Latin, Greek, Arabic, Hebrew, the law, mathematics, and theology; indeed, he took all of human knowledge as his province and set out to bring all that man had ever known into a single supreme system of thought.

Pico's energies often led him astray. He made the mistake of falling in love with a grocer's wife from Arezzo, and when the grocer died, the lady's relatives married her to a distant relative of Lorenzo's. Pico, nevertheless, decided to carry the woman off. With his secretary and twenty companions, he swept her onto his horse and galloped out of Arezzo. The town guards, meantime, raised the alarm and sent the constables in pursuit of Pico. In the melee that followed, fifteen men were killed, and Pico barely escaped with his mistress to a neighboring town, where he finally was arrested and jailed.

Informed of the affair, Lorenzo brought it to a diplomatic conclusion. It was unthinkable, he decided, that the wife of a Medici could be unfaithful to her husband; the abducted lady was returned to Arezzo as she so ardently— Lorenzo determined—must have wished. Pico, Lorenzo also decided, could not have been at fault; he must have been misled by his secretary. Pico thus was released, and his secretary was left to the constables to do with as they chose.

Of the many young scholars surrounding Lorenzo, Pico della Mirandola was among the brightest.

The far-ranging interests of Lorenzo's young friend Pico della Mirandola helped to stimulate a revival of Hebrew studies. A page from a Jewish manuscript by Jacobus ben Aser of Mantua depicts the slaughter and preparation—by bleeding—of animals according to Hebrew dietary requirements.

Once again, in 1486, Lorenzo had to rescue the hot-headed young scholar. Obstreperous as always, Pico had mounted a horse and gone to Rome, there to proclaim that he would debate no less than nine hundred separate propositions with anyone in the world. Unfortunately for Pico, Pope Innocent VIII appointed a commission to review the theses and decide whether any of them violated the teachings of the Church. Seven were found to be heretical, and six "dangerous." Pico picked up his books and fled to France, where he was arrested and jailed in the fortress of Vincennes. This time Lorenzo intervened through diplomatic channels, arranged for Pico to be released and brought back to Florence, and there provided him with a villa.

Pico's greatest contribution to the new humanist thought grew directly from his restless quest in all philosophies and religions for common truths. In his studies of Hebrew, and particularly of cabalistic writings, he found a doctrine of love, as opposed to intellect, that dovetailed nicely with Neo-Platonism. And with his ebullient scholarship, he managed—though not quite singlehandedly—to bring about a "Hebrew revival." One of his followers, a man named Reuchlin, was the first to publish a Christian-Hebrew grammar. Clearly, Pico had started something, and indeed, it was through him that an awareness of Hebrew thought began to influence the thinking of the Western world.

He published a small library of his own writings, and at least one of them must stand as a monument in the history of the freedom of human thought: *De Astrologia*, a tightly reasoned, vehemently argued attack on astrology that all but buried it in the annals of serious thought—although perhaps it never will be eliminated as a subject of popular study. Pico's life was almost as short as it was brilliant. He became, finally, fanatically religious, and he cloistered himself in a monastery—there to fast, scourge himself, and die in a blaze of scholarly work in 1494, at the age of thirty-one.

The leading poet of Lorenzo's group was Angelo Poliziano, whom we have encountered before as the tutor of

In company with scholars before and after him, Pico was unsuccessful in his attempt to discredit the widespread practice of astrology. The creator of this fifteenth-century miniature graphically asserted the influence of the heavenly bodies on earthly happenings.

Lorenzo's children. A thick-set man, with a huge, hooked nose, he was the leading Classical philologist of his day. It is said that he had so thoroughly mastered Greek and Latin that he not only wrote and talked the languages but actually thought in those tongues as well.

Poliziano was born in 1454 in the lovely mountain-bastion town of Montepulciano, near the southern end of the Chiana valley. Lorenzo found him, at the age of sixteen, living with an uncle in Florence. He had translated the first book of the *Iliad* into impeccable Latin hexameters. Lorenzo read it, instantly invited the young man to live at the Palazzo Medici, showered him with all the books he wanted, and finally installed him in a country villa.

Poliziano was made professor of Latin and Greek at the University of Florence, and his lectures were replete with wit and with irrelevant, fanciful discussions—for instance, in introducing a text by Aristotle, he talked about the power of witches. His vogue as a poet, however, was short-lived. Not long after Poliziano's death, literary critics rightly decided that his poetry, while technically sublime, was empty of meaning. He stands in some sense as a warning to all poets against the dangers of imitation, for he had imitated so perfectly the voices of the Greek and Roman poets that he had lost his own.

Yet there is one accomplishment that cannot be taken from Poliziano. He wrote occasionally in the "vulgar" tongue of Italian. Toward the end of Poliziano's life, Lorenzo, the greatest champion of the use of Italian in "high art," persuaded him to write more and more in the vernacular, and these later poems have something of a more relaxed charm about them. One of Poliziano's earliest works in the vernacular is quite remarkable. During a visit to Mantua, in the midst of the bustle of court festivities, he wrote *Orfeo* in Italian. Laced with lyrical melodies, it is the first Italian operatic drama, and Poliziano composed it in a few days.

Altogether, this group that gathered around Lorenzo was tremendously lively. At first Italy, and then much of Europe, buzzed with talk of its discoveries, its music and poetry, and its ideas. When the leaders of Naples and Milan decided to build palaces, they wrote first to Lorenzo to seek his advice on their design.

When a competition was held to design a new façade for the Duomo in Florence, Lorenzo himself shamelessly worked up a design to submit as his entry. The competition among the other twenty-eight entries was as formidable as can be imagined; it included the famous artists Botticelli,

Bernardo Poccetti's drawing was entered in Lorenzo's contest for a new façade for Florence's cathedral.

Ghirlandaio, Perugino, Filippino Lippi, and Verrocchio. Craftily, the commission appointed to choose the winning design turned to Lorenzo, the self-acknowledged amateur expert in architectural affairs, and asked him to decide the winner. But Lorenzo was no amateur in the ways of diplomacy. Perhaps he was a bit irritated because he could not bring himself to choose among the artists, all of whom were his friends; one suspects that his sly sense of humor played a part as well. For, rather than choose a design, Lorenzo

In his small, neat handwriting, Lorenzo wrote a novel, Giacopo, *which discussed certain of womankind's less attractive traits.*

had words of praise for all of them and then suggested that the decision be postponed. Postponed it was; the cathedral did not get its new façade for another three and a half centuries.

The Medici lavished money on learning and the arts. In his memoirs Lorenzo notes:

I find we have spent a large sum of money from 1434 up to 1471, as appears from an account book covering that period. It shows an incredible sum, for it amounts to 663,755 florins spent on buildings, charities and taxes, not counting other expenses, nor would I complain about this, for though many a man would like to have even part of that sum in his purse I think it gave great lustre to the state and this money seems to be well spent and I am very satisfied.

Precise modern equivalents for this sum would be hard to estimate. We know, however, that Botticelli might be paid, for one of his magnificent paintings, between fifty and one hundred florins, and a man might live for a year in relatively high style for only two hundred florins.

One of Lorenzo's greatest passions was books and manuscripts, which he bought from all around the world for himself and his scholars. In one year alone he spent thirty thousand florins on books and manuscripts. Two hundred Greek manuscripts, nearly half of them previously unknown in Italy, were brought back from Mt. Athos; mathematical works by Archimedes, commentaries on Plato, treatises on architecture, the writings of Caesar and Cicero, Vergil and Homer—all poured into the Palazzo Medici, to be read and talked about by the Platonic Academy over dinner at the Palazzo or while they all drank wine late into the summer nights around the small fountain in the garden of Lorenzo's villa at Careggi.

The group revolved around Lorenzo not merely because he was its patron. More important than that, he was its source of inspiration, its jovial, cynical, garrulous, rambunctious leader. And he was one of the group; he was a creator himself of songs and poems. He cannot be considered a great poet, but in retrospect, we can see that he easily surpassed the admired Poliziano. Where Poliziano, the good classicist, chose his Latin words carefully and penned his lines with an elegant balance and restraint, Lorenzo flung himself into his images with gusto and abandon, reveling in the sounds of the vernacular Italian and in the resonance of his metaphors—unconcerned whether they were strictly to the point or not.

Like the good Neo-Platonist that he was, Lorenzo wrote

OVERLEAF: *Humanism placed the cause of love high above that of war on its scale of noble values. In this fresco, from the Este palace in Ferrara, the war god Mars is humbled before Venus. At upper right is the garden of love, presided over by the three Graces. At the bottom are Taurus the bull and other astrological images.*

love poetry. And, while it must sound stilted to us now, there remains a freshness about it, as for instance, in one of his most famous quatrains from a carnival song:

> Fair is youth and void of sorrow:
> But it hourly fades away—
> Youths and maids, enjoy today:
> Nought ye know about tomorrow.

The song is a narrative of nymphs and satyrs cavorting with Bacchus and Ariadne, rounded out with a presentation of the aged Midas, who has wasted his years and found no pleasure in his life. The moral is repeated:

> Listen well to what we're saying;
> Of tomorrow have no care!
> Young and old together playing,
> Boys and girls be blithe as air!
> Every sorry thought forswear!
> Keep perpetual holiday—
> Youths and maids, enjoy today;
> Nought ye know about tomorrow.

As songs, Lorenzo's works must have had the same direct appeal (however much the sentiments may differ) that Bob Dylan has today. And he could, in another mood, be rather somber, even with the same theme:

> Lady, vain is the thought that dare not say
> That with the years old age will surely come,
> And youth has no sure home
> In which to bide for ever in one stay.

> Time's on the wing and flies;
> Soon from our life the blossom must depart:
> This thought must therefore stir the gentle heart,
> That everything is snatched by time and dies.

Just as Lorenzo's talents were myriad, so too were his moods, and he gave expression to them all. Not long after the deaths of his wife, Clarice, and his mistress, Lucrezia, he fell in love with a young married woman named Bartolomea de' Benci. Bartolomea's prim niece Ginevra (the subject of a portrait by Leonardo da Vinci) was shocked by the affair, so chagrined, according to one story, that she left Florence to live in the country. And Lorenzo, with his tongue tucked firmly in his cheek, wrote her a sonnet:

> As Lot flew with the daughters of his bed
>   Sodom in its prodigious conflagration,
>   His wife turning to view that just damnation,
>   A trunk of salt stood rooted in her stead.

The woodcuts reproduced on these pages illustrated published volumes of Lorenzo's songs. He appears prominently in each, as if to make certain that his songs are well sung—and with enjoyment.

So—by a prodigy of grace—you fled
    This town, this furnace of abomination:
    Go, gentle soul, a holy dispensation
    Forbids that you should even turn your head.

Our Good Shepherd in seeking you forsook
    Whole flocks for a lamb, and back to the fold
    Brought you rejoicing in his arms that day.

Eurydice, when Orpheus stole a look,
    Was almost free, but fell back in the hold
    Of Hell: so do not turn, Hell lies this way.

Nor did he neglect parody. He parodied Dante, and in an even more ribald poem, he parodied the Catholic sacrament of Confession:

Ladies and maids, myself I pass my sentence
On all my faults, and for them make repentance.

The faults Lorenzo confesses are his shortcomings as a lover; he repents not for his sins but for not having been a better sinner.

Peasant women picking spinach—as depicted in this herbal of the fifteenth century—was a familiar sight in the countryside around Florence. Some of Lorenzo's best poetry dealt with such simple pastoral subjects.

And then he wrote a play—a terrible play, an unspeakably bad play. Characteristically, it was packed with action, in which Lorenzo's sons, and perhaps Lorenzo himself, appeared. It was called *San Giovanni e San Paolo*, and Hollywood could do worse than to pick it up, for it has a banquet scene, two full-scale battles, a couple of religious conversions and political uprisings, and the miraculous cure of a leper.

In addition, the character of Constantine in Lorenzo's play is something of a mouthpiece for Lorenzo's ideas and ideals. He is, first of all, weary of being a ruler, a man who wishes that he could abandon politics for the good life of contemplation. But since he is ruler, he preaches that a king must rule for the good of all citizens, not for his own selfish desires, that he must be just, hold honor above all other virtues, neglect astrologers and shape his own course, be charitable and humane. He must, in sum, be a humanist.

Lorenzo's best writing is contained in three poems, all of them having to do with the country around Florence: *Ambra*, *Caccia col Falcone*, and *Nencia da Barberino*. *Caccia* concerns a day of hunting with hawks; *Nencia*, a peasant singing the praises of his mistress; and *Ambra* is a pure celebration of nature. In its best passages, like the one below, *Ambra* is somewhat reminiscent of such great poet-singers as Gerard Manley Hopkins:

Engraved against the sky, the shrieking cranes
Wheel—and in varied lines again unwind,
Each with outstretched neck his rank maintains
And in the air a marshal order is defined.

Because Lorenzo was patron and politician and poet, because he founded a university and a school of harmony for his friends and musicians, collected ancient gems and cameos for his own private museum, took an ardent amateur's interest in architecture, and because he zestfully took all of life and learning as his realm, we think first of him when we conjure up the image of the humanist. We think of him first when we invoke the archetypal Renaissance Man. Humorous and erudite, able to tell a ribald joke or to translate Homer, to grow grapes and rule a state, he and his friends gave their lives a breadth that expanded finally to take in the whole of the world. By the time they died, there was little of life that they had not experienced. With all their faults and lapses and excesses, the humanists of the Renaissance still must seem to us today to have defined an ideal type of human being.

REVOLUTION IN THE ARTS

Early in the fifteenth century, the architect Filippo Brunelleschi sat down on the steps in front of the central door of the cathedral in Florence to make a drawing. He was in his thirties at the time, not yet very famous, and he was an insatiable student of antiquity. Whether or not he had in mind an ancient Roman text when he set about to make his drawing is not clear. The modern historian Vincent Cronin believes that Brunelleschi was thinking of a passage from the Roman architect Vitruvius' work *On Architecture*, a treatise discovered by the Florentine humanists about 1410. In the seventh book of that work, Cronin points out, is the following passage:

Agatharcus, at the time when Aeschylus taught at Athens the rules of tragic poetry, was the first who contrived scenery, upon which subject he left a treatise. This led Democritus and Anaxagoras, who wrote thereon, to explain how the points of sight and distance ought to guide the lines, as in nature, to a center, so that by means of pictorial deception the real appearances of buildings appear on stage: painted on a flat vertical surface, they seem nevertheless to advance and recede.

On a thick wooden panel (about the size of this book) Brunelleschi made a drawing of the baptistery of San Giovanni, across the street from the cathedral. The drawing was unlike any that had been done since the time of Agatharcus; for on that board's flat, two-dimensional surface, Brunelleschi made the baptistery appear in three dimensions: solid, massive, as deep as it was tall and wide.

The principle that Brunelleschi had rediscovered was that of perspective, and he spoke of the discovery to a young friend of his, the painter Tommaso Masaccio. Masaccio, in

Ghirlandaio's fresco in the Sassetti chapel of the church of Santa Trinita depicts the founding of the Franciscan monastic order. At right, watching Saint Francis receive the papal bull, are Sassetti, who was manager of the Medici bank; his son; Lorenzo; and an unidentified fourth figure.

Two characteristics of painting in the Renaissance—emphasis on architectural detail and the use of one-point perspective—are apparent in Leonardo da Vinci's sketch, above, for his painting The Adoration of the Kings.

turn, applied the principle to a set of frescoes that he painted in the Brancacci chapel in Florence. From that time on, Western painting never was to be the same. Whereas the artists of the Middle Ages—like the painters of China, India, and Byzantium—had filled walls with flat, two-dimensional scenes, the artists of the Renaissance came to view their picture frames as though they were windows through which one could look on a countryside populated with substantial, fully rounded men and women, a spacious, three-dimensional world—real enough to step into.

To the Brancacci chapel, as to a schoolroom, came the men who created the Florentine Renaissance of the arts: Fra Filippo Lippi, Filippino Lippi, Andrea del Castagno, Verrocchio, Ghirlandaio, Perugino, Botticelli, Leonardo da Vinci, and Michelangelo. They pushed space back farther and farther from the window frame, molded it, shaped it, and gave color to its shadows. Leonardo da Vinci, with a technique called *sfumato*, infused the air itself with a palpable texture: his blurred outlines and pale colors caused his figures to melt dimly into a distant haze. At the same time, this new-found space was filled with strenuous action, with muscular bodies, with ancient heroes, with gods and goddesses. Out of the mists of a tradition that had exalted unearthly saints came a new kind of painting and sculpture—firmly planted in this world, with man triumphantly at its center—so irrepressibly alive that as Donatello sculpted his

The Florentine artist known as Masaccio made the Brancacci chapel of the church of the Carmine a pilgrimage center for many generations of artists. One of his series of frescoes there, The Tribute Money, *above, was among the first paintings executed in a fully matured Renaissance style.*

marble figure called *Lo Zuccone*, he is said to have muttered to it, "Speak, damn you! Speak!"

The artists of the Renaissance created a new notion of space, and of man's place in it, not only in painting but in architecture and sculpture as well. Brunelleschi, by reviving ancient principles in his own field of architecture, revolutionized that art and became the originator of what we now call the Renaissance style—an elegant, open style that is evident in the private houses and villas and churches of Florence's fifteenth-century building boom.

Another of Brunelleschi's friends, Donatello, did for sculpture what Brunelleschi and Masaccio did for architecture and painting. Donatello's greatest work symbolic of his place in this story is his bronze *David:* the first large freestanding nude sculpture done since antiquity. And it is doubly important because it was done for a private patron, Cosimo de' Medici, to celebrate a political rather than a religious idea: the arts had begun to leave the service of the Church. Less and less did they conjure up images of an afterlife; more and more did they exult over man's brief, strenuous life on earth.

Thus, these three men, at the beginning of the fifteenth century, opened a rich vein of gold; the story of art in Renaissance Florence is essentially that of the mining of that same vein, again and again, by the generations of artists that followed. In fact, it can be said with some truth

119

Vergil and Beatrice rise to Paradise in this Botticelli illustration of Dante's Divine Comedy.

that it took four hundred years to exhaust the riches of that vein. The course of art was not so fundamentally changed again until the debut of the Post-Impressionists of the late nineteenth century.

By the time Lorenzo was born, Masaccio had been dead twenty years, Brunelleschi three, and Donatello was an old man. There had been no "artists" at the beginning of the fifteenth century—only craftsmen; painters, whatever their merits, were treated as the lowliest of artisans. They did not even have a guild of their own but were relegated to membership in a division of the Guild of Apothecaries and Doctors. But by Lorenzo's time, artists had begun to sign their works. Their eccentricities were tolerated. While the title Creator formerly had been reserved to God, artists now spoke with infinite boldness of their creations.

Masterpieces abounded, and there were technical innovations at every turn. Cosimo had spurred some of the activity, patronizing Brunelleschi and Michelozzo and showering his largesse on sculptors. He gave Donatello myriad commissions, and when the sculptor became too old to work regularly, Cosimo gave him a pension. Lorenzo's father, Piero, was an enthusiastic patron of decorators and painters, giving commissions to Gozzoli, Uccello, and Pollaiuolo. (Piero, incidentally, seems to have been the most gauche of the Medici. Over a tabernacle built for him in the church of SS. Annunziata, he had inscribed the crass boast: "The marble alone cost 4,000 florins.") The arts were fully, vigorously—and sometimes vulgarly—alive. Lorenzo cannot be said to have started any of this. By his time, it would have taken an act of God to stop the artists of Florence.

What Lorenzo did do was help to shape the forces at work in Florence. He encouraged a number of men: Verrocchio, Bertoldo di Giovanni, Ghirlandaio. But the most telling influence he exerted can be seen best through the careers of two men, Botticelli and Michelangelo. To Botticelli, Lorenzo and his humanist circle gave the subject matter for his paintings; to Michelangelo, Lorenzo apparently gave a definition of art itself and an idea of its purpose.

Sandro Botticelli was born in 1444 or 1445—we cannot be certain of his birthdate—the youngest of seven children in a tanner's family. According to Giorgio Vasari, the painter, biographer of painters, and friend of Michelangelo, his father "brought him up carefully and gave him a good schooling. But although the boy learned readily what he wished to learn, he always was discontented and took no pleasure in reading, writing, or accounts." He was a frail

 BOTH: SPENCER COLLECTION, NEW YORK PUBLIC LIBRARY

120

and sickly child and a positively melancholy young man. His father, no doubt exasperated with the boy, turned him over to a goldsmith to learn that trade. There, Botticelli's elusive curiosity was captured by the jewels and gold and ornaments that he worked with, and there he learned to carve wild flowers like those that later would garland the women in his paintings.

From the goldsmith's shop Sandro wandered off to study for a time with Filippo Lippi and to pick up bits of technical skills from Verrocchio, Pollaiuolo, and Ghirlandaio. He continued to live in his father's house, near the home of the Vespucci family, and to paint there, as his father ruefully said, "when he felt like it." Then, when he was twenty-six years old, he finished his first signed picture for a series of paintings of the seven Virtues, a series begun by Antonio Pollaiuolo. Botticelli already had done several sad madonnas, and to complete Pollaiuolo's Virtues, he painted a cold, dismal rendering of Fortitude.

He never married, whether out of shyness or a wish to be free to devote himself entirely to his art we cannot discern. It is said that Tommaso Soderini once tried to convince Botticelli to marry and that Botticelli responded by telling Soderini of a nightmare he had had: "I dreamed I had married, and that caused me so much pain that I woke up. I was so frightened of dreaming the same dream again that I spent the whole night walking round Florence like a madman, so as not to sleep."

The source of this story of Botticelli's dream is Poliziano. Like most writers, Poliziano loved a good story more than he loved a fact, and his tale may well reflect that bias. Yet all fiction contains some truth, if not in its particulars then in the way in which it reveals something about the men who make it up and enjoy it. Stories of the high-spiritedness of Renaissance painters abound; another typical one was told of Botticelli by Vasari—who was, like Poliziano, a connoisseur of lively tales.

In another drawing from the Divine Comedy *series, the tormented in Hell are bound in iron chains.*

A weaver set up eight noisy, clattering looms in the house next to Sandro's. The painter could not work; he could not even stay at home. When he asked for an end of the disturbance, the reply was that the weaver both could and would do as he liked in his own house. Sandro then balanced an enormous weight of stone on the roof of his house that was higher than his neighbor's. This stone threatened to fall when the wall was shaken, and had it done so it would have crushed the weaver's roof, floors, looms, and workmen. The man hastened to Sandro in terror but got the same reply he himself had given: that Sandro both could and would do

In his Adoration of the Magi *Botticelli included likenesses of three generations of Medici. The old kneeling king is Cosimo; Piero wears a red cape; the proud, sword-bearing figure at left probably is Lorenzo.*

as he liked in his own house. Thereafter the weaver became a less troublesome neighbor.

Just how Botticelli came to meet the Medici is unclear. Perhaps his neighbors the Vespucci introduced him, since it was rumored that Simonetta Vespucci and Giuliano de' Medici were lovers; or less romantically, Pollaiuolo may have introduced the young painter to Lorenzo. In any case, about 1475 Botticelli produced his first truly splendid painting, the *Adoration of the Magi*, in which the principal members of the Medici family can be recognized: Cosimo, although he had died by the time Botticelli was commissioned to paint the picture, appears at the center, the kindly, eldest king, with a patrician profile; to the right is Giuliano, handsome, serious, wearing a black cape; at the extreme left stands Lorenzo, shoulders thrust back, a princely look of near-disdain on his face, calmly, confidently resting on one foot as he surveys the proceedings. And at the extreme right, Botticelli has painted his own self-portrait. This is our first glimpse of the artist, and he seems to have grown into an attractive young man. He is about thirty years old at this time, with a sturdy, thick neck, hefty shoulders, and good, clear eyes. He has turned to look at us, as we gaze at the religious event, and his expression is one of slight distaste, as though he resents our intrusion.

With this painting, at a single stroke, Botticelli had "arrived," and the expression on his face seems to indicate that he knew he had. Subsequently, except for a brief sojourn to Rome to paint several scenes in the Sistine Chapel for Pope Sixtus, Botticelli settled down in Florence and became the painter to the Medici. After Giuliano was killed in the Pazzi conspiracy, Botticelli painted several portraits of Lorenzo's younger brother; and when Lorenzo returned from Naples, having ended the Pazzi war, Botticelli—as we have seen—commemorated the event with a painting of Pallas and the Centaur, representing rule through suasion rather than force.

Like Poliziano and Vasari, Botticelli, too, loved a good story, and his most famous paintings are interpretations of the myths, expounded to him by the members of the Platonic Academy, surrounding Venus, goddess of love. Botticelli, it has been pointed out frequently, was the link between the arts and the letters of Renaissance Florence.

To understand his paintings, it is necessary first to understand something of what Venus meant to the Neo-Platonists. As goddess of love, she was at the very center of that new philosophy-religion of love. She was the symbol of

peace and of harmony, and of course, of regeneration or rebirth. Moreover, she was, for the men of the Platonic Academy, a figure who united the philosophical world of the
academy with the spiritual world of the Church, for one of
her accompanying symbols, as we see from Botticelli's *Birth
of Venus*, was the scallop shell, an early Christian symbol of
the rising soul. The Neo-Platonists were greatly enamored
of such unifying notions as this; we can recall that Pico della
Mirandola aspired to acquire all human knowledge and
unite it in one harmonious whole.

Perhaps Pico or Ficino or Lorenzo encouraged Botticelli to suggest the other image that springs to mind in looking at *Birth of Venus*: Christianity's male counterpart to
Venus. The composition does recall the baptism of Christ—
a naked figure against the water, with angel-like Zephyrs
hovering above. The Christian scallop shell further points
up the parallel. Here, then, are united Platonic and Christian beliefs, and on the most fundamental level, the painting simply evokes that synthesis and states that love is the
central force of life.

Perhaps, too, if we may guess further at Botticelli's
meaning, the painting had an even more immediate message for Lorenzo and his friends. They may have seen in this
figure rising from the sea, about to step onto the garlanded
earth, their conviction that a new age had been born. Botticelli seems to have understood that this new man-centered
age, cut off somewhat from the certain Christian promises
of salvation, was to have a dark as well as a bright aspect.
He has given Venus a curious expression of mute tragedy,
an awareness that she brings not only rebirth, but sorrow
and pain, too. One might improvise endlessly on the nu-
ances of meaning contained in the *Birth of Venus*, but the
central meaning is straightforward enough.

Botticelli's *Primavera* is quite another case. It is difficult
to know precisely what was going on in any artist's mind
when he set about to paint. Because Botticelli was so er-
ratically moody, it is even more difficult with him. Added
to that is the confusion of the Neo-Platonist ideas that inspired him, and the fact that few critics have been able to
resist the tempting notions that can be found in *Primavera*.

The most popular theory is that Venus, also at the center of this painting, is Simonetta Vespucci, Giuliano's re-
puted mistress, and that Mercury, at the left, is Giuliano
himself. Cupid, presumably, is aiming his shaft at Chastity,
one of the three Graces. And on the right, Zephyr, the chill
wind of early spring, is clutching at the earth-nymph

Chloris—suggesting, somehow, impending tragedy. Chloris, in turn, apparently is metamorphosed into the flower-be-decked Flora, intimating rebirth arising from the tragedy. All this would indicate that the painting is a celebration of a love affair between Giuliano and Simonetta. Since it was painted in 1477 or in 1478, the year in which Giuliano died and two years after Simonetta had succumbed to consumption, the meaning of the note of tragedy is unmistakable.

The mood of *Primavera* often is compared to that of a poem by Poliziano, memorializing a joust held several years earlier in honor of Giuliano and at which Simonetta was the Queen of Beauty. Slender as this connection is, the poem is thought to have inspired, at least in part, Botti-

These details from Primavera reveal the skill with which Botticelli—the most Classical-minded of the Renaissance painters—mastered human form and expression. Flora, goddess of Nature (right), is lovely and innocent, but not without a certain impish sophistication. The Graces, below, are more serious—almost efficient at the business of being graceful.

celli's painting. It is a lovely theory, but unfortunately, there is not a shred of evidence to support it.

The painting was done for a young cousin of Lorenzo's, and it is probable that it was based upon a letter written to the young man by Marsilio Ficino. If that is true, then the painting, like *Birth of Venus*, is meant once again to illustrate the doctrines of the Neo-Platonists. The personages remain the same, according to this theory, and as an Italian critic recently wrote, the painting is "an allegory of the kingdom of Venus, of an ideal world where nature and instinct, embodied by the erotic Zephyr and Flora, are ennobled by culture and civilization, embodied by Venus (Humanity) accompanied by the Graces." The basic notion probably was elaborated upon by Lorenzo or Poliziano; one can imagine, for instance, that the trinity of characters to the right represents beauty (Flora) emerging from passion (Zephyr) and chastity (Chloris)—an idea that would have come from Poliziano's readings of the Classical poets.

In any case, Lorenzo's friends were not inclined to settle upon one rigid interpretation of a work of art and insist that it have a single meaning to the exclusion of any other. Indeed, while there is no evidence to support it, there is little reason to suppose that Lorenzo's friends, looking at the painting, did not see in it the story of Giuliano and Simonetta—just as so many people have done since then. It would have been characteristic of these men of free-wheeling imaginations, who so loved to unite one story with another.

Botticelli's paintings are intriguing puzzles to gaze at and to make up explanations for, but of course, his reputation as a painter does not rest upon mystery alone. His first and most lasting appeal has been described by the modern critic Bernard Berenson:

If we are such as have an imagination of touch and of movement that it is easy to stimulate, we feel a pleasure in Botticelli that few, if any, other artists can give us. . . . imagine an art made up entirely of these quintessences of movement-values, and you will have something that holds the same relation to representation that music holds to speech—and this art exists, and is called linear decoration. In this art of arts Sandro Botticelli may have had rivals in Japan and elsewhere in the East, but in Europe never. . . . The representative element was for him a mere libretto: he was happiest when his subject lent itself to translation into what may be called a linear symphony.

Toward the end of his life, after the death of Lorenzo, Botticelli's melancholy claimed his spirit entirely. He became a convert to the reforming, hell-fire and brimstone

Ever concerned with the subject of birth—be it the birth of Christ or of a new season—Botticelli painted his most famous canvas in 1485. Birth of Venus, *above, is a celebration of the birth of the goddess of love.*

friar Savonarola. He ceased to paint his lovely women, reportedly burned some of his drawings of nudes, and lost faith altogether in the bright promise of Lorenzo's Florence. Finally, he stopped painting. He died at the age of sixty-six, a reclusive, decrepit, and lonely man.

In 1488, concerned that there were no sculptors in Florence comparable to the painters, Lorenzo apparently determined to form a school for promising young sculptors. It is said that he set aside the Medici Gardens, a small, enclosed private park near the monastery of San Marco, and there he placed a number of the antiquities that he and his father and grandfather had collected. The garden was, in fact, the world's first museum, and it contained an impressive array of statues, stone columns and capitals, portrait busts and funerary urns. He placed the old sculptor Bertoldo di Giovanni in charge of the school, and he turned to Ghirlandaio for recommendations for his first students.

Ghirlandaio had among his students a remarkably precocious fourteen-year-old boy, Michelangelo Buonarroti, the son of a local magistrate. Either through natural gifts or tutelage, Michelangelo already was an accomplished sculptor; he had grown up near the stone quarries of Carrara and could handle a hammer and chisel before the age of ten. He was taken into Lorenzo's school straightaway, and according to Vasari, he tried his hand first at some work in terra cotta. He "was so successful that he was given

ORSANMICHELE, FLORENCE

The fourteenth-century Florentine relief above shows the close quarters in which pre-Medici sculptors, having no prestigious position, had to work. At right, a manuscript of a century later depicts an artisan worthy enough to have his own workshop and an occasional visit from the god Mercury.

SPENCER COLLECTION, NEW YORK PUBLIC LIBRARY

μέγαι·

τίνι τὰ μεγάλα μέλιτος ἐκχύσαν-
τος, μέγαι πρὸς τὰ δειχθ᾽ ἀν᾿
ἐκπεσόντων δὲ τῶν ποδῶν αὐτῶν, ἀ-
ναστῆναι οὐκ ἔχων. ἀποπνιγόμε-
νᾱ ἐλέγον, ἀθλίαι ἡμεῖς, οἳ διὰ βρα-
χεῖαν ἡδονὴν ἀπολλύμεθα ·· ὁ τὸ
ὁ μῦθος δηλοῖ, ὅτι πολλοῖς ἡ λίχν᾿
τᾱ τῶν κακῶν αἰτία γίνεται ··

θρενᾶς καὶ ἀγαλματοποιὸς·
ἑρμῆς ποτε γνῶναι βουλόμενος ἐν
τίνι τιμῇ παρ᾽ ἀνθρώποις ἐ-
στὶν, ἧκεν εἰς ἀγαλματοποιοῦ, ἑαυ-
τὸν εἰκάσας ἀνθρώπῳ· καὶ θεασάμε-
νος ἄγαλμα τοῦ διὸς, ἠρώτα πόσου τις
αὐτὸ πρίαιτο ἂν ἀνοῖται· τοῦ δὲ, εἰ-

a piece of marble to work on. He began to copy the head of a marble faun, a Roman work. He changed it, opening the mouth wider to show all the teeth. The Magnificent [Lorenzo] was delighted with it." Lorenzo, so the story goes, joked that he did not think an animal as ancient as this old faun would have such perfect teeth. Michelangelo, missing the jest, picked up his chisel again, "broke out a tooth and even filed down the gum to make it look shrunken. Lorenzo was much amused."

The result was that Lorenzo decided to take Michelangelo into his household. As another contemporary recounts it:

"Go," he said [to Michelangelo], "and tell your father that I wish to speak with him." Michelangelo accordingly went home, and delivered the message of the Magnificent. His father, guessing probably what he was wanted for, could be persuaded only by the urgent prayers of Granacci [a young art student] and other friends to obey the summons. Indeed, he complained loudly that Lorenzo wanted to lead his son astray, abiding firmly by the principle that he would never permit a son of his to be a stone-cutter. Vainly did Granacci explain the difference between a sculptor and a stonecutter: all his arguments seemed thrown away. Nevertheless, when [the father] appeared before the Magnificent, and was asked if he would consent to give his son up to the great man's guardianship, he did not know how to refuse.

Again, all these stories must be read skeptically; modern scholars doubt that the incident of the marble faun ever occurred, and certainly the true story of Michelangelo's taking up residence at the Medici palace was not so quick and simple. Yet somehow Michelangelo did attract Lorenzo's attention, and he lived in Lorenzo's home for four years, until Lorenzo's death in 1492. There were shaped much of the character and talents that one day would earn for him the epithet the Divine Michelangelo. He became—this uneducated, barely literate, but vastly gifted young man—a great master not only of sculpture, but of painting, architecture, and poetry as well. No other man has attained such brilliance in all four of these arts.

Living as he did in the home of the most versatile Florentine of his time, Michelangelo took for granted the idea that he should try his hand at all the arts. Lorenzo treated him as one of his own sons; in fact, Michelangelo's companions were Lorenzo's son Giovanni and Giuliano's son,

This muscular torso was but one of thousands of anatomical sketches that Michelangelo made in advance of his many marble masterpieces.

Opposite, an admirer's portrait of the Divine Michelangelo. As a youth, the fiery genius had lived at the Medici palace for four important years.

133

During the Middle Ages most art had been commissioned by and for the Church. In the fifteenth century, however, the Medici became leading patrons; as a result, other aristocratic families began to buy works of art as status symbols. With the Church's continuing support, artists and artisans enjoyed a period of great activity, and in many cases, prosperity. Scribes, such as Francisco d'Antonio del Chirico, who made the Book of Hours pictured on the opposite page (upper left) for Lorenzo, found work executing manuscripts for private customers. Makers of functional utensils also were called upon to make elaborately decorated objects, such as the jasper jar with a silver base and lid, which also belonged to the Medici. Cosimo de' Medici commissioned the fresco at left of Christ and the Apostles for a cell at the convent of San Marco; the artist was Fra Angelico, who, with another monk, Fra Filippo Lippi, painted the exquisite Adoration of the Magi *above, purchased for Lorenzo's superb art collection.*

Giulio, the future popes Leo X and Clement VII, who one day would commission a good many of Michelangelo's works. He was given an allowance and clothes and a good room in the palace, and most importantly, he was given a regular place at the dinner table, where he could absorb the conversation of Lorenzo's friends.

From Poliziano and Cristoforo Landino, Michelangelo learned Dante, and after some time, he had committed the whole of Dante's *Divine Comedy* to memory. The great poem left its permanent impress: the influence of Dante's imagery can be seen clearly in Michelangelo's *Last Judgment* in the Sistine Chapel. It was at that time, with the encouragement of Lorenzo and the other members of the Academy, that Michelangelo began to write poetry himself.

All Lorenzo's friends "paid him particular attention,"

The two relief sculptures reproduced on these pages were executed by Michelangelo while he worked in the Medici garden. Madonna of the Stairs, *at right, was carved in 1491, before the artist was seventeen. A year later, he fashioned* The Battle of the Centaurs, *opposite. In the later work the incredible sense of body-strain and movement characteristic of his mature style already can be observed.*

the sixteenth-century painter and Michelangelo disciple Condivi wrote, "and encouraged him in the honorable art which he had chosen. But the chief to do so was the Magnificent himself, who sent for him oftentimes in a day, in order that he might show him jewels, cornelians, medals and suchlike objects of great rarity . . ."

Michelangelo's first works in marble were executed in Lorenzo's sculpture garden. The very first was a rectangular plaque, the *Madonna of the Stairs*, and despite all its faults, Michelangelo's promise is undeniably present. The second, probably suggested to him by Poliziano, is the *Battle of the Centaurs*. It, too, was a sculpture in relief, and it is bursting with the tortuous muscularity that makes so many of Michelangelo's great sculptures intensely, restlessly vital. Michelangelo himself must have had a special affection for this work, for he kept it with him all his life.

His greatest works were done, of course, many years later, long after Lorenzo had died and after Michelangelo had left the Medici palace. Yet by the time he left the palace, all the instincts and most of the skills that were to make him one of the most dazzling artists ever to live were well on their way to full flower.

Aside from these few works of art—the dozen or so paintings by Botticelli that are closely connected with Lorenzo, and the few early sculptures of Michelangelo—precious little in the way of tangible objects can be traced to the patronage of Lorenzo. It is said that he gave some commissions to Filippino Lippi and Ghirlandaio, but nothing has survived of their supposed work for him at one of his country homes. He utterly ignored the incomparable Leonardo da Vinci, and there is no satisfactory explanation for that oversight. Yet Leonardo was notorious for beginning stupendously challenging projects and then abandoning them as soon as he had satisfied himself that he was capable of mastering the challenge. That trait alone may have been sufficient to turn Lorenzo from him.

The perplexing fact remains that remarkably few works of art survive to support the illustrious reputation Lorenzo had in his day as a patron of the arts. It is, on the face of it, a disturbing and embarrassing situation, and it has misled a good many modern scholars to such conclusions as "the apparently commanding role of Lorenzo de' Medici as great patron was partly the result of later Medici propaganda."

The key to the enigma of Lorenzo's reputation lies, however, not in propaganda, but in the fact that we have forgotten what art was before his time. His idea of art most decidedly has made its impression: we take it so much for granted that we forget that it ever has been any different.

Before Lorenzo's time, as we have seen, art was intended to commemorate holy days, to summon up the sacred images of the saints, and later to memorialize one political event or another. But Lorenzo believed, as apparently he taught Michelangelo, that a beautiful work was worthwhile in its own right, that it had its own existence, to be appreciated for itself, as were Michelangelo's first sculptures. In short, he believed in art for art's sake. As an idea, Lorenzo's conception must have astonished his contemporaries. It has served assuredly to liberate artists ever since. If he originated it, as it seems plausible that he did, that would account for his reputation. And if he did, we must rank him with Brunelleschi, Donatello, and Masaccio as the fourth great revolutionary force in Renaissance art.

Carved from a long, scarred piece of marble that several other sculptors had rejected, Michelangelo's David *was completed in 1504 and instantly became a symbol to the Florentines of the strength and vigor of their city.*

Church as much as in it. Thus, Lorenzo invited to Florence the agent of his own destruction.

Savonarola arrived in the city in 1489, and his manner in the pulpit was harsh, violent, and terrifying. He roared of God's impending revenge on Florence for its reprobate ways. He foretold deaths and famines and plagues, of invasions and wracking calamities that would befall the unrepentant. And he called up the images of a hell broiling with the screams of tormented sinners. Thousands flocked to his sermons and overflowed the church where he preached. Pico, Ficino, Poliziano, Botticelli—all came to hear, to tremble, and to believe. Sixty years later, Michelangelo would say that he still could hear ringing in his ears that chilling, direful voice.

As Florence lost confidence in its newfound dreams and the old nightmares of anxiety welled up again, Lorenzo succumbed more and more to the ravages of gout. He was seen less and less frequently in Florence as he took refuge at the soothing baths in the neighboring countryside and at his own peaceful villas. He sought solace once again, as he had so often before, in the pleasures of his orchards and fields, in his books, in the company of his friends and of his family.

With the growing realization that he soon was to die, he prudently provided for the futures of his children. His daughter Lucrezia was married to a Salviati; Contessina, to a Ridolfi. Maddalena was married to Francesco Cibo, the son of Pope Innocent VIII. Piero, who would become head of the family, was allied to his mother's family, the Orsini. The youngest, Giuliano, would have to wait until after his father's death before marrying into the family of King Francis I of France.

Because Lorenzo realistically appraised Piero as an unreliable young man, it was to his son Giovanni that he looked with greatest hope for the future of the Medici. Having ingratiated himself with the Pope through the marriage of Maddalena, Lorenzo managed to have Giovanni appointed a cardinal at the age of fourteen. He was, as Lorenzo noted proudly, not only "the youngest of living cardinals, but the youngest that has ever existed," as well.

Lorenzo was too ill to be present at the celebration of

Like the gentlemen in the manuscript illustration at left, Lorenzo visited the baths in the countryside near Florence, seeking relief from gout. Hoping that his son Giovanni (above) would maintain the Medici leadership, Lorenzo had the youngster ordained as a cardinal at the age of fourteen.

The rantings and ravings of the fanatic monk Savonarola—as depicted at right by an admirer, Fra Bartolomeo—had a terrifying and even paralyzing effect on Florentines. Nevertheless, as the woodcut on the opposite page suggests, they flocked to hear of their impending damnation. Coined in 1497, the bronze medallion at far right reflected one of the monk's predictions: God's hand, clutching a dagger, descends on Italy.

Giovanni's investiture. In the early spring of 1492 he was carried to the villa at Careggi, where both his father and his grandfather had gone to die. There Poliziano stayed in constant attendance, and the doctors gave Lorenzo their usual remedy for a great banker: "various precious stones . . . pounded together in a mortar."

As Giovanni set out for Rome, however, Lorenzo wrote him a letter of encouragement and advice.

I know [he wrote fondly to his son], as you are now going to Rome, that sink of all iniquities, that you will find some difficulty in following [virtuous paths], as bad examples are always catching, and inciters to vice will not be wanting. Your promotion to the Cardinalate, as you may imagine, at your age . . . will be viewed with great envy, and those who were not able to prevent your attaining this dignity will endeavor, little by little, to diminish it by lowering you in public estimation and causing you to slide into the same ditch into which they have themselves fallen, counting on success because of your youth. You must be all the firmer in your stand against these difficulties, as at present one

sees such a lack of virtue in the College. I recollect, however, to have known a good many learned and good men in the College, leading exemplary lives. It will be well that you should follow their example, for by so doing you will be the more known and esteemed as being different from the others. . . .

You know how important is the position and the example of a Cardinal, and the world would be far better if the Cardinals were what they ought to be, for then there would always be a good Pope, from whom emanates, one may say, peace for all Christians. Make every effort, therefore, to be this; if others had done so we might hope for universal good. . . .

Lorenzo failed quickly now, and toward the end, he sent for a priest to make his last confession. Another final visitor was his nemesis, Fra Savonarola. The two men never had met before. Instinctively recognizing each other as enemies, aware that their antagonism could be resolved only by the death or defeat of one of them, they had stayed apart, cautiously stalking one another for three years. Now Savonarola came.

To [Savonarola's] exhortations to remain firm in his faith [Poliziano recorded], and to live in future, if God granted him life, free from crime, or if God so willed it to receive death willingly, Lorenzo answered that he was firm in his religion, that his life would always be guided by it, and that nothing could be sweeter to him than death, if such was the divine will. Fra Girolamo then turned to go when Lorenzo said: "Oh Father, before going deign to give me thy benediction." Bowing his head, immersed in piety and religion he repeated the words and the prayers of the friar . . .

Thus was their mutual antagonism resolved in the ritual of the Church.

On the night of April 5, out of a clear and calm sky, a thunderbolt lashed down at the cathedral of Florence.

The lantern of the cupola . . . was struck . . . [Luca Landucci reported], and it was split almost in half; that is, one of the marble niches and many other pieces of marble on the side toward the door leading to the *Servi*, were taken off in a miraculous way; none of us had ever in our lives seen lightning have such an effect before. . . . This marble niche fell and struck the roof of the church . . . and broke the roof and the vaulting in five places, finally fixing itself in the brick floor of the church. And many bricks and much other material from the vaulting fell also. . . .

It was considered a great marvel, and [significant] of some extraordinary event, especially as it had happened suddenly, when the weather was calm, and the sky without a cloud.

On Sunday evening, April 8, 1492, Lorenzo died at the age of forty-three. "It was said," Landucci wrote, "that when he heard the news of the effects of the thunderbolt, being so ill, he asked where it had fallen, and on which side; and when he was told, he said: 'Alas! I shall die, because it fell toward my house.' This may not have been so, but it was commonly reported."

His body was taken to the old sacristy of San Lorenzo, where it was laid next to that of his brother, Giuliano, under the sarcophagus that had been built for their father and grandfather.

After Lorenzo's death, Piero ruled Florence—haughtily and ineptly—until 1494. Then the king of France crossed

The fifteenth-century illustration above shows the death of a nobleman of Florence. Lorenzo de' Medici's own death came just before the golden age of the Florentine Renaissance was consumed by Savonarola's graphic oratory. Below is Lorenzo's death mask.

the Alps with his army, to fight for an ancient French claim to Naples. Piero met him, bowed to him, and returned to Florence in humiliation only to be driven from the city by the disillusioned and angry Florentines, who felt themselves betrayed. The Medici palace was sacked, its paintings and sculptures and jewels trampled and scattered by the raging mobs.

In 1494 Savonarola began a fleeting and ugly rule of the city, taking out on it the revenge of a bitter puritan. But in 1498 the mob turned on him, too, and amid raucous jeers they hanged and burned him at the stake.

Not until 1512 were the Medici restored to power in Florence—at the hands of Giovanni, soon to be Pope Leo X. But the rule thenceforth was to be a cheerless despotism. The city now was the shroud of its former self.

After Lorenzo's death no one appeared to re-establish the balance of power. There came more invasions, twice more by the French, and also by the Austrians, the Germans, the Swiss, the Flemings, the Hungarians, and finally —conclusively—by the Spaniards.

The artists were gone from Florence. No more great architects grew up to adorn the city with churches and homes. No longer were there sculptors who could fashion "the Gates of Paradise." No longer did the gardens of country villas buzz with excited talk of Plato, with confident hopes of mastering all human knowledge and uniting it in one resplendent whole. Never again would Florence be nearly so magical. Never again would the Florentines call any man Magnificent.

Lorenzo and his beloved Florence flowered and died together. Their lives were brilliant—and brief.

ACKNOWLEDGMENTS

The Editors would like to thank the following individuals and organizations for their valuable assistance:

Biblioteca Casanatense, Rome
Biblioteca Estense, Modena
Biblioteca Vaticana, Rome
Cleveland Museum of Art, Cleveland, Ohio
Philip Foster, Florence
Myron P. Gilmore, Director, Villa I Tatti, Florence
National Gallery of Art, Washington, D.C.
New York Public Library, Prints Division—Elizabeth Roth
Pierpont Morgan Library, New York
Nicolai Rubenstein, Warburg Institute, London
Scala, Florence
Miss Bianca Spantigati, Rome
Mrs. Maria Todorow, Florence

The quotations on pages 13, 63, 77, 85, and 146 are from *A Florentine Diary from 1450 to 1516*, by Luca Landucci, published by E. P. Dutton & Co., Inc., and reprinted with their permission. The quotations on pages 16 and 17 are from "Changing Attitudes Toward the State During the Renaissance," by Garrett Mattingly, published in *Facets of the Renaissance*, © 1959 by University of Southern California Press, reprinted by Harper Torchbooks, 1963. The quotations on pages 17, 68, and 75 are from *The Medici*, © 1949 by Ferdinand Schevill, published by Harcourt, Brace & World, Inc. The quotations on pages 24, 42, and 45 are from *Lorenzo de' Medici*, by Edward Armstrong, published by G. P. Putnam's Sons, 1923. The quotations on pages 27–28 are from *The Italians*, © 1964 by Luigi Barzini, published by Atheneum Publishers. The quotations on pages 40–41, 102, 117, 121, and 143 are from *The Florentine Renaissance*, © 1967 by Vincent Cronin, reprinted by permission of E. P. Dutton & Co., Inc. The quotations on pages 57 and 60 are from *The Civilization of the Renaissance in Italy*, by Jacob Burckhardt, published by Harper & Brothers. The quotation on page 84 is reprinted with permission of The Macmillan Company from *Daily Life in Florence*, by J. Lucas-Dubreton, © 1961 by Librairie Hatchette, Distribué par Presse-Avenir. The quotations on pages 90, 92, and 93 are from *The Rise and Decline of the Medici Bank 1397–1494*, by Raymond de Roover, © 1963 by the President and Fellows of Harvard College, published by Harvard University Press. The quotation on page 109 and the excerpts from Lorenzo's songs on pages 112 and 113 are from *Italian Renaissance Studies*, ed. by E. F. Jacob, © 1960 by Faber and Faber Ltd., published in the U.S. by Barnes & Noble, Inc. The quotations on pages 120, 121, and 123 are from *The Essential Vasari*, ed. by Betty Burroughs, © 1962 by Unwin Books, reprinted by permission of Simon & Schuster. The quotation on page 127 is from *The Italian Painters of the Renaissance*, by Bernard Berenson, © 1952 by Phaidon Press, London, distributed in the U.S. by Frederick A. Praeger, Inc. The quotations on pages 130, 133, and 136–137 are from *The World of Michelangelo*, by Robert Coughlan and the Editors of Time-Life Books, © 1966 by Time Inc. The quotation on page 138 is from *Early Renaissance*, © 1967 by Michael Levey, published by Penguin Books Ltd.

The quotations on pages 97 and 99 are from *The Portable Renaissance Reader*, ed. by James Bruce Ross and Mary Martin McLaughlin, © 1953 by The Viking Press, Inc. Also from *The Portable Renaissance Reader* are the following: the quotations on pages 87 and 88 are reprinted by permission of Harvard University Press from *Florentine Merchants in the Age of the Medici*, by Gertrude R. B. Richards, published 1932; the quotation on page 102 is reprinted by permission of *Journal of the History of Ideas*; and the quotation on page 141 is reprinted by permission of Ernest Benn, Ltd.

FURTHER REFERENCE

Readers who are interested in viewing examples of Renaissance art and artifacts will find collections at the Bowes Museum, Barnard Castle; Blackburn Museum and Art Gallery; the Fitzwilliam Museum, Cambridge; the National Gallery of Scotland, Edinburgh; Glasgow Museum and Art Gallery; the British Museum and the Victoria and Albert Museum, London; Manchester City Art Gallery; the Whitworth Art Gallery, University of Manchester; the Ashmolean Museum, Oxford; the Uffizi Galleries and the Galleria dell' Accademia, Florence; the Louvre, Paris; and the Museo del Prado, Madrid.

For those who wish to read more about the Renaissance in Italy, the following books are recommended:

Armstrong, E. *Lorenzo de' Medici*. Putnam, 1923.

Barzini, L. *The Italians*. Hamish Hamilton, 1964.

Berenson, B. *The Italian Painters of the Renaissance*. Phaidon, 1959.

Burckhardt, J. *The Civilization of the Renaissance in Italy*. Phaidon, 1965.

Burroughs, B., ed. *The Essential Vasari*. Allen & Unwin, 1962.

Coughlan, R. and the Editors of Time-Life Books. *The World of Michelangelo*. Seymour Press, 1968.

Cronin, V. *The Florentine Renaissance*. Collins, 1967.

De Roover, R. *The Rise and Decline of the Medici Bank 1397–1494*. OUP, 1963.

Ferguson, W. K., *et al. Facets of the Renaissance*. Harper & Row, 1963.

Gilmore, M. P. *The World of Humanism, 1453–1517*. Harper & Row, 1952.

Horsburgh, E. L. S. *Lorenzo the Magnificent and Florence in her Golden Age*. Putnam, 1908.

Jacob, E. F., ed. *Italian Renaissance Studies*. Faber & Faber, 1967.

Ketchum, R. M., ed. *The Horizon Book of the Renaissance*. New York: American Heritage, 1961.

Landucci, L. *A Florentine Diary*. Translated by A. de R. Jervis. New York: Dutton, 1927.

Levey, M. *Early Renaissance*. Penguin, 1967.

Lucas-Dubreton, J. *Daily Life in Florence*. Translated by A. Lytton Sells. Macmillan, 1961.

Machiavelli, N. *History of Florence and of the Affairs of Italy*. Harper & Row.

Medici, L. de'. *Tutti le Opere di Lorenzo de' Medici*. 3 vols. Biblioteca Universale Rizzoli, 1958.

Ross, J. B. and McLaughlin, M. M., eds. *The Portable Renaissance Reader*. New York: Viking, 1953.

Ross, J., ed. and tr. *Lives of the Early Medici as Told in Their Correspondence*. Gorham, 1911.

Schevill, F. *History of Florence*. Constable. *The Medici*. Harper & Row, 1963.

Vasari, G. *Lives of the Artists*. Translated by E. L. Seeley. Allen & Unwin, 1960.

Young, G. E. *The Medici*. New York: Modern Library, 1930.

Scholarship and craftsmanship dominate the routine of daily life in Flor-ence, according to this fifteenth-century manuscript illustration—a depic-tion of the city functioning efficiently under the influence of Mercury.

INDEX

Boldface indicates pages on which maps or illustrations appear